UNIVERSAL SYMPHONY

Author
Professor Dr. Yelda Ozsunar

Translated by
Fatma Balci Kaya

I0169112

Edited by
Doreen Martens

Publisher
Cosmo Publishing

Cosmo
Publishing
Company

ISBN 978-1-949872-08-8

Science and art desert the land that does not appreciate them.
Ibn-i Sina (Avicenna)

UNIVERSAL SYMPHONY

A guide with scientific literature, poetry and tales for self-healing

Writer: Professor Dr. Yelda Ozsunar

Translations of text from Turkish to English: Fatma Balcı Kaya

Translations of poems: Yelda Özsunar and Fatma Balcı Kaya

CONTENT

The doctor of the future will give no medication but will interest his patients in the care of the human frame, diet and in the cause and prevention of disease.

Thomas Edison

PROLOGUE

For centuries, the brain has been the human organ that garners the most interest. This big object in our heads, which looks much like a walnut, is at the helm during our body's journey through life. It is constantly influenced by the environment; it develops, changes and is sometimes deceived; it has the power to heal or, through thoughts and emotions, to make the body ill. It is the most crucial component of our identity and our journey through life. Many volumes have been written trying to explain the mysteries of the brain and delving into the scientific research on neuroscience. These books must be revised and amended every few years in response to the copious amounts of information that come out of new research. Even a medical doctor can be confused and overwhelmed in the face of it all. Efforts to explain the intricacies of the brain will continue for centuries.

The fact is that our brain is able to select the information that benefits us, to retain experiences that will give us pleasure, and forget the rest. It lops off superfluous information in the same way that one prunes a tree and relegates the bits it deems redundant and unnecessary to oblivion, well-hidden in the mysterious nooks of the brain.

As physicians and scientists, we delve deeper into the intricacies of neuroscience and sometimes get lost in the sea of scientific knowledge. We may not be able to convey important information to our patients and others in plain language they will understand. But healing is a process in which a physician and patient need to communicate in terms both can comprehend. To begin with, everyone should understand and know their own body; protect their own body, with the guidance of science and observation; and contribute to their treatment as much as their physician does.

Everyone should be aware that medical science has established principles that will help the body combat stress, protect it from illnesses, aid healing, and form the basis of a healthy, balanced, and happy life. Modern treatment methods are more effective when patients are aware of these precepts, are well-informed, and embrace responsibility for their own health.

The unhealthy and polluted environment many people live in, as well as an unhappy and vacuous way of living devoid of aesthetic values, can lead to illness. It turns many an individual into a client of the system we might call "mechanical medicine," which prescribes standardized treatments: the same medications and surgical procedures to every patient. The importance of empathy between a patient and her physician, the fact that the medical profession is an art, differences in personalities of patients, and the particular living conditions of a patient are frequently overlooked.

Yet, just as every snowflake is unique, every human being is special and different from others, despite our commonalities. For this reason, each patient should receive a doctor's focus, like a tailor making a custom-made outfit, and be given enough time for an individual analysis. However, the time a physician devotes to each patient has been declining, due in part to increasing costs and overcrowding of medical facilities.

The purpose of this book is to combine my medical observations, which primarily relate to the brain—the mysteries of which I've been probing throughout my career—with knowledge and experience firmly rooted in science, to raise awareness in society about how to attain a healthier life and methods that aid healing. Every chapter contains a story aimed at drawing attention to fundamental information, which I call *science in a nutshell,* that I hope will inspire and motivate readers to take an interest in their own health and science.

In the first of thirteen chapters, I'll draw analogies between the sea of waves filling the universe, called the electromagnetic spectrum, and a musical symphony, and between the human brain and an instrument that contributes its own vital part to an orchestra as it performs a piece of music. In the following chapters, the basic functions of the brain and body, especially our sensory organs, which receive the waves of the electromagnetic spectrum, are summarized, along with nuggets of interesting information and useful examples from current literature.

It has been claimed that in our times the information we are exposed to in a daily newspaper is equivalent to a lifetime's worth of acquired knowledge in the 17th century. It is not possible for a normal human brain to process and remember this excessive amount of information, most of which is unnecessary or repetitive. For this reason, taking as my starting point that excessively detailed information is a burden for the normal person, I've included in the *science in a nutshell* section only the filtered information I thought would be most useful to an individual. If interested, the reader can cultivate the relevant scientific information provided in a nutshell by researching the sources I've provided and by expanding it with the aid of keywords on the Internet or print material. I believe that core information that is absorbed and internalized is the best kind of knowledge. Learning this information is important, but equally so is remembering it. Research on learning and neuroscience has shown that the degree to which a person retains and internalizes information and experience is proportionate to the intensity of feelings the information evokes, as well as whether the information is based on real stories or observations and the extent to which it is useful to the person. Therefore, I tried to make recalling the information easy by including a "story and an observation" section reflecting on real events, which I hope will help readers tap into their own internal feelings and thoughts and help them retain the information.

Though it's unusual for a scientist and physician to choose poetry as a means of communication, my love of literature and any written form of art, combined with my curiosity for learning and science, as well as my passion for the beauty

4

of life and my quest to help people to stay alive, impelled me to such an endeavor.

To sum up, I believe my primary duty as a physician is to protect people from illnesses without harming them. The source of our complaints is not illness itself but adverse living conditions, insufficient awareness of our own body, lack of understanding of its language, and our inability to take the necessary precautions. As a physician, I believe it is wrong to be a mere intermediary in the transit between life and death, merely a medium to delay death, to be the prescriber and the servant of expensive technologies. For these reasons and owing to my admiration for the human will and body, I would like to convey my many years of experience and observations regarding illnesses as a physician, and as a photographer of the brain and body, using an interdisciplinary and holistic approach, along with recommendations for treatment. It is my desire to convey this message through an alliance of science and art, as was suggested by Ibn-i Sina (Avicenna).

I hope this book is read, understood, felt, enjoyed, and benefitted from.

INTRODUCTION TO THE AUTHOR AND THE BOOK

Professor and Medical Doctor Yelda Ozsunar Dayanir is a renowned academic in the field of radiology. Her quest to understand life better and to make it more pleasant, as well as her scientific research, renders her a truly universal scientist. In this book Professor Ozsunar applies to her medical research a multidisciplinary approach and synthesizes it on a more emotional plane: to utilize the tools of art to look at it from a different perspective.

In this regard *Universal Symphony* is not a textbook for medical students: it is a book meant to appeal to old and young alike. Information pertinent to our well-being, be it commonly known or not, is analyzed, explained, and questioned from an aesthetic perspective.

The first four chapters of *Universal Symphony* delve into the functions and working of the brain, the enigmatic organ that steers our body as well as how the thought process works. Relying on scientific knowledge, Professor Ozsunar endeavors to show us in unconventional ways how our brain affects our perceptions, emotions, thoughts and behavior. With stories she utilizes art's ability to make emotional connections.

Professor Ozsunar wants to impress these ideas upon the reader, consciously and subconsciously, using real-life stories and visual pictures. Professor Ozsunar has penned *Universal Symphony* in a way that enriches scientific data with an emotional perspective. Moreover, with Professor

Ozsunar's creativity, this exploration of the human brain, the body's immune system, DNA, and genetic structure almost turns into a scientific symphony.

In later chapters, Professor Ozsunar scientifically explains how stress, a phenomenon that affects all of society, as well as fear, breathing, smell, and touch each affect our body. While using an artistic approach in her explanations, Professor Ozsunar also emphasizes the importance of music and visual arts in how patients are perceived, how they help in decoding their problems, and how they affect the recovery process.

Professor Ozsunar uses a lyrical style in bringing together a complex and interdisciplinary subject. In *Universal Symphony,* the reader will witness how a scientific book can express and evoke emotions and will identify with the content personally. I wish all readers a pleasant time reading this book and congratulate Professor Yelda Ozsunar on writing it.

Professor of Fine Arts Meltem SOYLEMEZ

The one who solves the mystery of vibration
solves the mystery of the universe.
Nicola Tesla

1 - UNIVERSAL SYMPHONY WITH THE WAVES

Folding Fan

While a fan
Vibrates silently the universe
A source of love is dispersed
As enigmatic waves
Attach the one to the whole
Passing through each boundary wall
For those who believe they are part of all
To let them hear the love call

There is a constant symphony playing in the universe. The scientists call this the *electromagnetic spectrum or electromagnetic fan*. This symphony is like an alphabet, formed of the waves that vibrate at every point of the universe. Every creation of the universe becomes a part of this symphonic orchestra and part of an immortal dance, forever…

Sound is just one letter of this alphabet of the vibrating spectrum; music is just a syllable. All animals, plants and humans recognize and understand this syllable. It is the common language of the universe. It swings and dances in the air, flows in from our ears; creates sparks in the brain and beats in our hearts. It rouses our soul, awakens our cells: it heals. All ears and hearts that hear it are aligned with one rhythm; all feelings are spread out into the universe; they become comprehensible in every being that can sense.

Beans grow faster, cows produce milk quicker, children understand faster, patients heal quicker when they join the dance of the universe. Listening to the symphony of the universe, joining in the dance of vibration, unites us, and raises us to the consciousness of union.

Scientists observe the universe; they play games with it in their experiments. With experiments they question the effect of the vibration of music that hits humans: the constant data transmission of the enigmatic box called the brain, which connects to the universe just like a radio receiver.

They have discovered how music is sensed not just by the ear but by the whole body; how each organ in the body has a favorite tune and how it heals when this tune is played. And how these sounds cause mysterious electrical discharges in the brain called alpha, beta, gamma, and theta waves, putting humans in bizarre emotional and physical states. How also our brains are in harmony with the symphony in the universe, sensing the waves and emitting waves in their turn.

And various other stores of knowledge, growing with every seed of curiosity…

Picture 1.1: 'An artistic illustration of Universal Symphony' S. Aydin

Science in a Nutshell

What is the electromagnetic spectrum?

The electromagnetic spectrum is the sum of all types of energy, in the form of waves, that exist in the universe. The spectrum includes many different types of waves, such as the sound we hear, the light we see, and those used by the radio we listen to, the TV we watch, and the microwave oven we use for cooking (1). These vary from long waves, as in radio waves, to short waves, smaller than the size of an atom, such as gamma rays (IPicture1.2). Sound waves are a form of waves in the electromagnetic spectrum, quite like radio waves in terms of wavelength and energy.

We, as humans, can sense a very narrow section of this universal spectrum with our sensory organs. Only one-trillionth of the electromagnetic spectrum (2), in fact! Only low-energy waves such as sound and light can be sensed with our sensory organs. The human ear can hear only the range between 20 hertz and 20 kilohertz. The human eye can see only light with wavelengths between 390nm and 750 nm (1-3). For example, the human eye cannot see ultraviolet light. We are not even aware of other waves we make use of regularly, such as X-rays, microwaves, gamma rays, and the waves used by mobile phones and other wireless connections.

Other living beings on Earth sense different ranges of this spectrum. All living beings, even viruses, communicate with each other using their own methods, using letters of this alphabet. Birds, butterflies and bees can see ultraviolet light that humans cannot see. Cats, dogs, bats, whales and dolphins can hear waves much higher than the range humans can hear. For instance, bats have the ability to hear sounds at 200 kHz, which humans cannot hear. In other words, they communicate among each other in a language that we cannot sense (1-3).

High-frequency waves (X-rays and gamma waves) that we cannot sense with our sensory organs can be harmful to our body. However, these waves become useful in radiologic methods of medical science, using techniques such as ultrasonography, magnetic resonance imaging, and computer tomography. Radiologists use machines that employ these techniques to take images of the body and illnesses affecting it, which physicians then interpret.

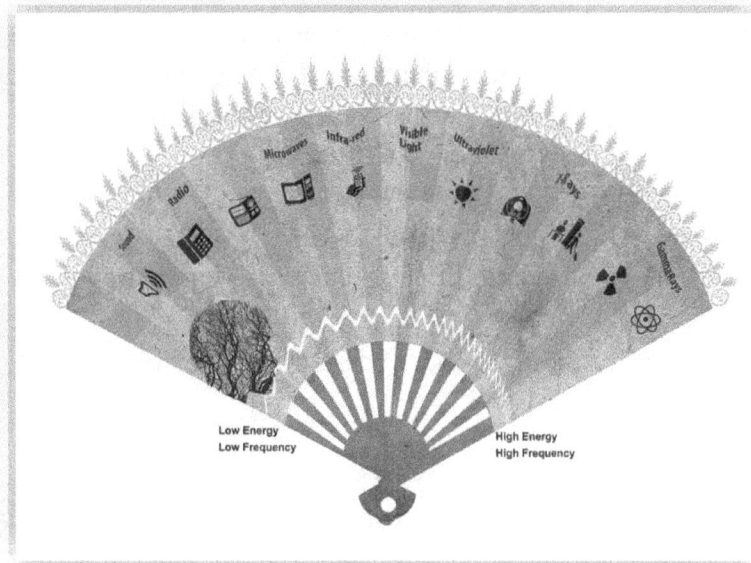

Picture 1.2: "Electromagnetic Spectrum" is represented as a folding fan

Does the human brain produce waves?

The recording machine called the electroencephalogram (EEG) is used to diagnose neurological illnesses, by measuring the electrical activity of the brain in various conditions; in other words, it measures the change in voltage caused by ionic movement (4). The electrical activity measured by an EEG is produced by millions of nerve cells in our brains. The cells, using the electrical energy produced, connect within themselves and the universe.

By producing different electrical signals in the following situations, the brain regulates the functions of the brain and body. These electrical signals are measured in hertz and are defined as being within the slowest range, with the lowest energy waves, within the electromagnetic spectrum.

In a normal person these waves, ranging from fastest to slowest, are the beta, alpha, theta and delta waves, each detected by standard EEG machines. Gamma waves are detected by more specialized EGG machines. The properties of these waves are described below [Picture 1.3] (4-7).

Beta waves (fast activity: 13 Hz or above): These are mostly detected when a normal person, with eyes open, is in a social environment, excited, and stressed, and the brain's stimulating factors and intellectual function are active. These waves are known to be linked to academic success and does not exist in a newborn. The source is mainly the frontal lobe of the brain which is responsible from our higher cognitive abilities. Beta waves start to develop at around 6 months to 2 years old. Being in a crowded environment, having numerous stimulants, solving problems all of these have the effect of increasing the beta waves. The brain works faster, the ability to concentrate increases. If there is an excessive increase in the beta activity that lasts a long time, the body secretes a hormone called adrenalin, typically during stress and flight. High levels of energy are used. The condition we call stress

14

overtakes the body. In such conditions, we have a propensity to be anxious and hyper-alert. Unwanted thoughts, insomnia and addictions begin to form. All our muscles contract. If substances such as caffeine, amphetamine and cocaine are used, anxiety increases. This state can be triggered artificially by methods such as Transcranial Magnetic Stimulation (4-9).

Alpha waves (8-13 Hz): They are mostly observed when a person is awake but relaxed, with eyes shut. These waves are usually generated in the occipital lobe. They disappear when the eyes open. They can be observed in low-level meditation. They decrease activity in the cortex. Intense mental concentration, tiredness, problem-solving, stress, and emotional and physical stimulants destroy the rhythm of the alpha waves (4-10). Mental stimulants also decrease the alpha rhythm. It is claimed that serotonin, dubbed the happiness hormone, increases during this alpha rhythm. When we take deep breaths, close our eyes, and focus inwardly, and during the hypnosis alpha waves start to increase. In relaxed and deep meditation conditions, these waves turn into theta waves. The brain waves gradually slow down and the entire body starts to relax and repair itself. Peacefulness and wellness spread to the body, memory function strengthens, remembering becomes easier (10). Music, audiovisual and rhythmic stimulants, yoga, antidepressants, relaxants, and stimulation with various technological brain waves all increase the alpha waves (9-11). Alpha waves are linked to a decrease in feelings of pain and anxiety (8,10). High level of cortical activity decreases. In contrast, the links between neurons, memory, and the ability to recognize words increase, and the individual feels calmer (9,10). These waves have a similar frequency to the electromagnetic waves called the "Schumann Resonance," which occur naturally on Earth.

Theta waves (4-7 Hz): These are waves normally detected when feeling sleepy. They are more prominent than alpha waves in children until the age of four. After the age of 5 or 6, alpha waves begin to occur more frequently. Theta waves are also detected during deep relaxation, when feeling sleepy and during the dream phase of sleeping. They increase with deep and fast breathing. Their intensity decreases with age. They are observed more during the eye-movement phase of sleep. It is thought that theta waves released when the eyes are closed put the person in the creativity condition called hypnogogia, and that they are detected more in creative, artistic people and musicians. It is also thought that they provide a link with our subconscious, remediate memory function and can help cure conditions such as post-traumatic stress disorder (11-15).

Delta waves (4 Hz and below): These are detected during deep sleep. They are very slow waves. No muscle or eye movement is observed during this phase of sleep. It is thought that delta waves increase the release of developmental hormones such as melatonin, DHEA, which is an anti-aging hormone, and growth hormone. They all have a positive effect on the immune system, thus contributing to the curing of illnesses. Continuous alpha and theta activity and, rarely, delta activity is detected in those who engage in deep meditation while awake. Delta waves are said to be more frequent in newborns, small children, and those diagnosed with attention deficit and hyperactivity disorders. Links have been established between medications such as ketamine and brain-derived neurotrophic factor (BDNF), which contributes to healing of the brain with the slowing of brain activity (11-16). It has been shown that such slow wave activities strengthen the brain's synaptic balance (the connectivity between neurons), thus helping in the treatment of brain damage (16-18).

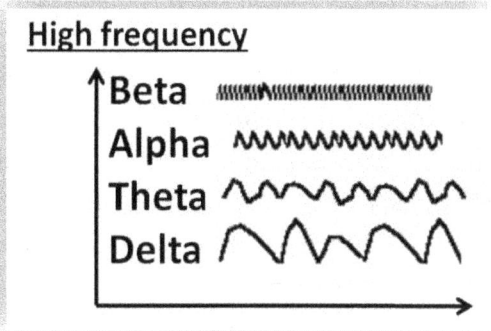

Picture 1.3: visual representation in a graph of the EEG waves emitted by the brain

A Story and an Observation

Every illness is an upheaval, a warning in the body's own language; so was Ayse's.

On that Monday morning, as was the case every day, Ayse woke from a deep sleep, where she was wandering among delta waves, by the ringing of the alarm clock. Thanks to this human invention, her body moved quickly from a calm state of happiness to a state of stress and alarm. She had to prepare quickly to go to work. Though her body did not want to leave the bed, the fast pace of the beta waves commanded the body to get up and get ready!

Ayse had to wake up. She had to make it to the meeting. Her brain needed to leave the delta state immediately and let the beta waves take over.

She got up and put the coffee on. Washed her face. Her body calmed down a little bit with the splash of water. Her brain was no longer furious with the clock that woke her up.

The smell of coffee wafted into the morning; she watched the sun rise as she sipped from her cup. Once again, her brain handed over command to the king cortex, called consciousness. She had to leave subconsciousness and its pleasures aside, to let the body take on the world and press on with the daily competition. She had to win and be successful. Her ego was whipping her body to get moving: *Come on, get going. If you're late, people won't like you, you'll be a failure ...*

She got ready and went out to mingle in the city's crowds, all physically close but keeping their distance emotionally, packed into groups and feeling trapped within the urban environment. People darted in and out of doors incessantly, pouring into the crowded streets in pursuit of their daily responsibilities.

Towards evening, when her body threw itself back into its little corner of the world, away from the crowds, Ayse found herself out of fuel. Her body was tired of fighting, her muscles were tense. Even the threads of her genes had shrunk. Her subconscious self was rebelling against the dimming of her soul. Her body, which she had ignored all day, was expressing its pain to the universe, in hopes that its owner was listening.

But her conscious brain, ignoring the deliciousness of her dinner, was preoccupied with what had happened that day, what had been said and experienced. It continued to suppress the body's weak voice. Ayse was busy dealing with a universe of thoughts dominated by her urge to always be on top of things, successful, and admired.

The body had been forgotten amid her tempestuous daily life. But all at once, Ayse's life toppled like a rock that begins rolling down a hill uncontrollably, becoming an avalanche of reactions until her body started to scream from pain. An illness appeared, forcing her to steer the wheel in a different direction. Ayse found herself in a hospital. She let herself sink into the white sheets, so she could rest.

While the body parts that had darkened were severed from her body by the hands of a surgeon, her eyes remained closed in the waiting room between life and death. The desires of her consciousness remained quiet for a while. Life and body sank into a deep sleep. She slept and slept. The sleep satiated the body and soul. On the stage of the subconscious, from which consciousness is banished, the soul and body played for a long time. Both the consciousness and the body grew stronger, until they were ready to meet the light.

One morning, a soft light touched Ayse's eyes. Outside appeared a big rainbow that looked like it was about to jump in through the big windows of the white hospital room. Ayse winked at the people who were lovingly waiting for her and said, "What a wonderful welcome!" She understood, once again, that she was not alone and that this experience was an enigmatic message, telling her wisely, "You have to change, now!"

Her brain, tired by the beta waves, stopped using her body as a slave for her ambitions. She started listening to the universal symphony quietly. She listened to the miraculous whispers of her own breathing. Her body started to rock slowly from one side to the other with a deeper awareness of the universe. She started to play her own fiddle, inspired by small ripples, meanings, coincidences, breezes, the chirping of a bird and the color of life.

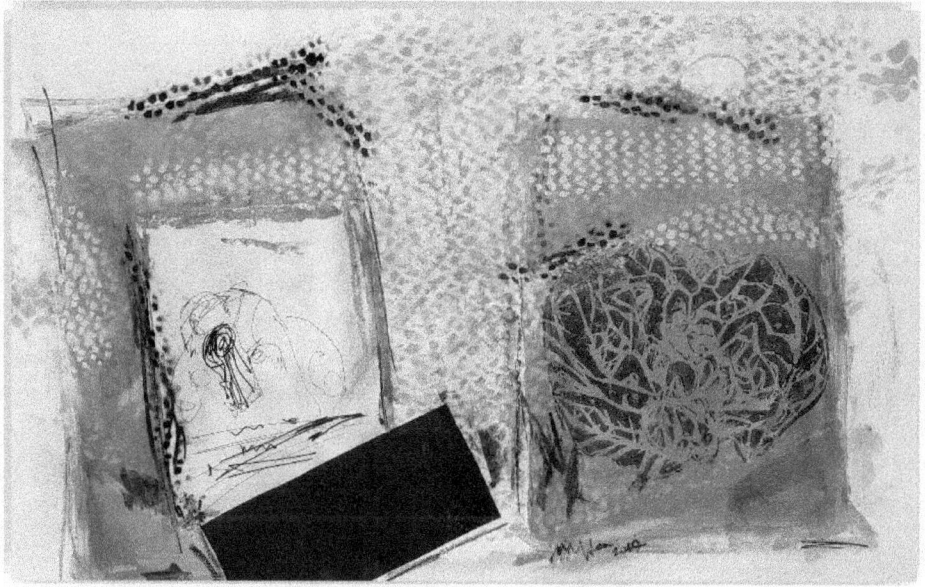

Art Picture 1: M. Söylemez "Illusion of the brain"

My brain is a mere receptor. There is an essence in the universe from which we get knowledge, power and inspiration. I haven't been able to penetrate the mysteries of this essence. But I know it exists.
Nicola Tesla

2- THE MIND AND BEYOND

Mind and Beyond

While the universal symphony
Is conducted in harmony,
Infinitely and timelessly,
I feel its signals endlessly.

When I see a rainbow
Through my tiny window
The Rainbow becomes a signal flare
For my mind in despair, for my body to repair

My every attention and emotion
Are reflected in the song's notation
I feel the joy and in me alteration
Then the beauty of the creation,

We are all bound together, not desolate
As a violin, our thoughts resonate
Our mind becomes a part of the symphony
My heart beats as a part of the harmony

Science in a Nutshell

What is the brain, and how does it work?

In its simplest and most basic definition, the brain is a computer, something like a biological machine formed of cells, called neurons, that receive and send signals, and cables, called axons, linking these cells. These cables are the arms and legs of the cells, called neuronal cells, which are responsible for transmitting signals (Picture 2.1).

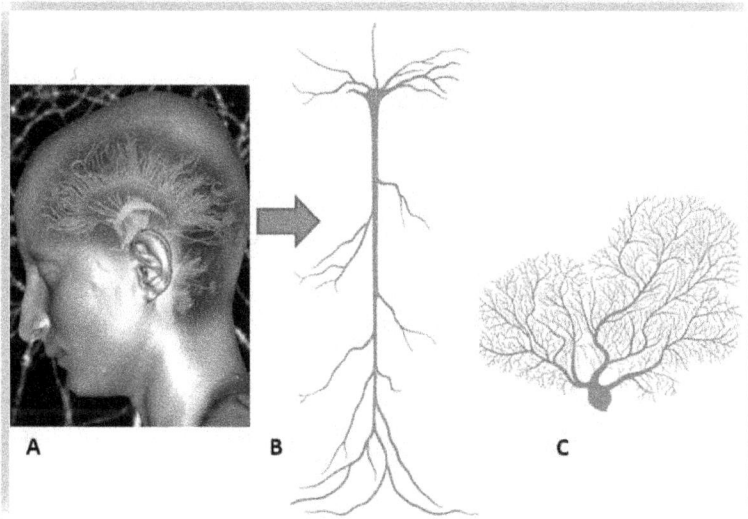

Picture 2.1: An MRI method called tractography represents the branches of the neurons. Samples of brain neurons or nerve cells (B. cortical and C. cerebellar nerves look like a tree)

The brain and the body receive and process information from the universe (the macro environment), just like the Internet or a radio receiver.

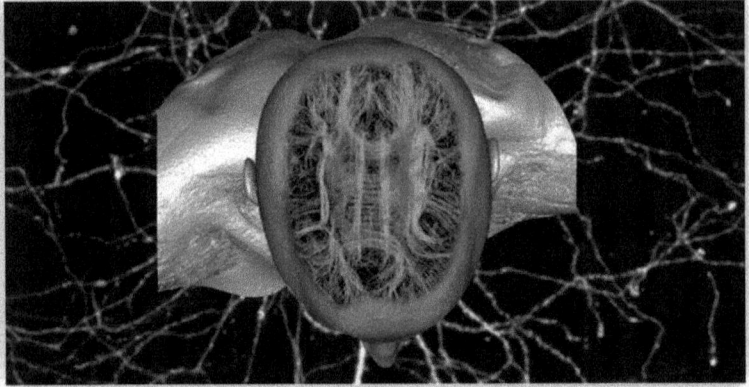

Pictures 2.2: Graphic design made by combining images obtained by the Magnetic Resonance Imaging (MRI) method called Tractography and Computer Tomography (CT).

The links in the white matter of the brain, which look like cables, are called axons and can be seen with magnetic resonance imaging.

The five senses that use the elements of the electromagnetic spectrum, such as visible light and sound, play the most important role in our awareness of this information. From the moment it is conceived in the mother's womb till its death, every brain interacts with and is reshaped by the genetic codes passed on by our ancestors and life experience. While there is pruning of presynaptic neuron connections, in long-term learning, where information is recorded in the memory, dendritic thorns are formed in the postsynaptic neuron connection (Picture 2.3). This dynamic process defines sense, memory, personality, point of view, and similar personal characteristics. (2-4)

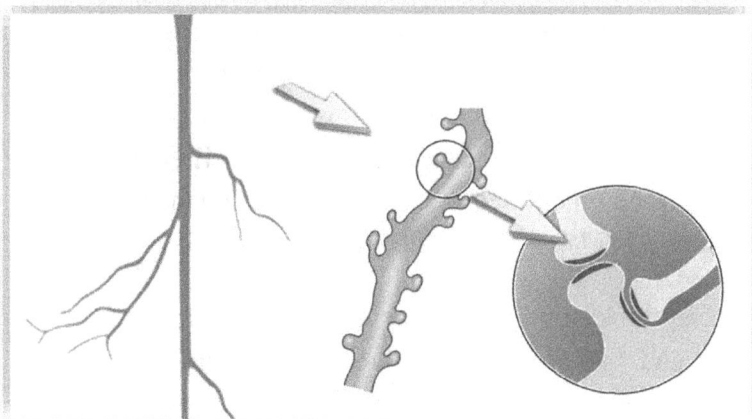

Picture 2.3: Illustration of connection types of dendritic thorns of neurons. The neuron cables are linked together with links called synapses.

Just as every snowflake is different from another, every brain and body are unique. Unlike the computers produced in a factory, no brain is quite the same as another in detail. It constantly renews, improves, ameliorates or causes damage to itself, sometimes to the extent that it no longer works. With the right training and conditioning, the capacity of the brain can be increased (4,5).

Like a radio receiver and transmitter, the brain sends and receives signals as part of the electromagnetic spectrum. While radio waves have a frequency between 50 and 1000 Hz, brain waves, although they have ups and downs, transmit signals from the scalp at frequencies between 10 and 120 Hz (6). When we focus on a thought, we produce energy at a certain frequency by the discharge of hundreds of axons. The wave produced by the brain at a specific frequency can interfere with another wave of a similar frequency. Although these waves produced by the human brain and body are of a very low strength, they can be measured with magnetoencephalography (MEG) and EEG and can be integrated by Magnetic Resonance Imaging (Picture 2.1) (7).

We can think of neurons as being something like computer chips and batteries that produce signals and energy and axons as the cables that transmit voltage signals. As a battery each neuron produces approximately 70 mV potential differentiation during rest. By creating signals that remove this potential differentiation, it is possible for a person whose arms and legs are disabled to regain command of her limbs after external chips are placed in the cortex of the brain (9).

A significant part of the information we compute from the external environment is produced by the activities of this complex network in our brains. Since no two brains are alike in terms of their complex network structure, our senses and thoughts are very special products produced by this machine. This is the product of the genetic codes hidden in our DNA and interaction with our environment.

Our DNA constantly changes due to environmental and living conditions. Using images and words, the brain can modify itself, the body and even the genes by producing emotions and thoughts (11-15). Feelings of anger and negative thoughts, for instance, suppress the frontal lobe and, with the help of the amygdala, which is related to fear and anger, cause the release of stress hormones. This leads to illnesses by suppressing the immune system or causing it to work irregularly. In reverse effect, the same brain can cause the release of hormones such as serotonin, which improve the immune system. This hormone is calming and happiness-inducing, contributing to the harmonious working of all cells and the immune system, as well as healing (11-15).

Much research has shown that learning, thinking, and meditation can cause structural changes in the brain and in our DNA. For instance, an increase in density was observed in the relevant parts of the brains of those who played the piano, learned mathematics or meditated. Learning a new language is as good as taking medication for Alzheimer's disease. This is because learning prompts the appearance of new cables (axons) in the brain, with the gaps between being filled with brain cells. In reverse effect, bad memories and traumas cause damage to the brain and the body by causing the release of stress hormones. However, this damage can be repaired by psychotherapy as well as a healthy social environment and stimulants (11-16).

In summary, the human brain forms a small unit of the universe as a receptor and transmitter, which constantly changes while interfacing with the environment. The bioenergy transmitted to the universe, created by the thoughts and emotions of humans, is among many examples of the low-frequency part of the universal spectrum (17). It is possible, with today's technology, to measure and change these frequencies and consequently contribute to the diagnosis and treatment of conditions (18).

A Story and an Observation

Stroke

I'm giving a lecture explaining stroke to medical students.

"You all know someone who had a stroke. Everything happens in a flash, within minutes. All a sudden, a blood vessel in the brain gets blocked or starts bleeding. The brain shuts down the parts that get affected by this extraordinary situation for a while. This is akin to an earthquake."

My mind drifts to the Canakkale earthquake, which I'd heard about on the news in the morning. The students are quiet and pensive, like me. What are those people who cannot go back into their houses doing now? What if stronger earthquakes follow?

I have to fend off the worries that cross my mind and focus on the lesson. I continue: "Shortly after a stroke the immune system cells rush to the location of the stroke, just like the aid teams arriving at the earthquake zone and start cleaning and repairing the area. The brain swells all of a sudden and it looks as if the condition has worsened. This lasts until everyone gets used to the situation and the cleaning and rescue teams finish their jobs. Then normal life resumes.

The immune system cells leave the disaster zone. Now it is time for the brain to recover and repair itself. The brain regains the steering wheel with the aid of a feature called plasticity; with the power of the will it repairs and heals itself, even if it is only a partial recovery. Life goes on, even if it is slightly different from the previous one..."

The lesson ends, and we take a break. I go to the canteen to drink tea, while the students are elsewhere. It's only myself and a female student named Filiz in the canteen. We greet each other and sit at our respective tables. The news is showing on a television hanging high on the wall; it's all about terrorism again, but today the earthquake is added.

While I'm drinking my tea, Filiz shrinks into a corner, watching the news. She is weeping, tears already rolling down her cheeks. I get up and go near her. I put my hand on her shoulder and sit next to her. Her eyes become bleary. "Professor, I can't stop thinking about my family in Canakkale. What if something happens to them? What if there are more tremors? I'm scared of losing them. I can't stop worrying to focus on the class. I get palpitations. All I want to do is cry."

I hold her hand and say, "Do whatever you feel like doing." "But first of all, focus on yourself and your own body. Calm it down. Recurrent fearful thoughts consume your energy and body. As you go over and over them, you feed the fear in your brain, and after a while you cannot overcome them. The brain has a fixed capacity for focusing consciously. When you think negative and scary thoughts, as an antidote you have to have pleasant thoughts. I read the story of a father who was trapped under the rubble for 48 hours and lost his spouse and one of his children. The father explained how, despite being injured, he survived his entrapment under the rubble by having the will and desire to live because of his 5-year-old daughter who was trapped with him. In order not to leave his daughter alone in life, he took control of the consciousness ship and resisted his fears. The power of love and affection inspired his will to live.

Just as this father did, you need to take the helm of your own ship. Your love for the ones you love should lead you not to fear but to acting with purpose, determination and perseverance. First take control of your thoughts; focus on positive things. Don't let your body suffer. And don't forget, all suffering is meant for learning and change. Not for cursing and feeling upset. Ignorant societies, instead of getting on with life, constantly accuse each other and fight. Civilized societies, which act with reason, focus on the solution. Humanity cursed smallpox for many centuries and suffered from it until science and reason discovered its cause and invented a vaccine. We go through difficult experiences in order to change, to become civilized and to follow the path of reason and scientific thinking to advance and make life better. And don't forget, no reality is as scary as the fears you envisage and magnify in your brain. Thoughts and imagination exaggerate all fears. Let me tell you a childhood memory: when I was a child, vaccinations were done at schools. When doctors and nurses turned up at school in an official vehicle with massive bags, the entire school would be hit with a wave of terror. Some of us shivering, some of us crying out of fear of needles, we waited for our turn. When suddenly the people in white coats burst into the classroom, the children scattered everywhere, and the teachers held their arms while the white-coated medical people stabbed in the injection. The way I dealt with the fear while I was waiting for my turn was to accept the terror of the needle that was waiting for me. When it was my turn to get the injection, the white-coated one inserted the needle in my arm. I didn't feel anything more than a faint insect bite.

"Is that it?" I asked.

"Yes, that's it," they said.

Moreover, the needle wasn't as big as I thought it was. The reality was much less scary than the fears my imagination had so magnified. In effect, the torment I endured while waiting for the injection was much greater than the torment I had when I got the injection."

We got up from our table with smiles on our faces, and we were late for the lecture. However, we were both feeling lighter because of the relief we'd experienced by sharing our emotions and talking about them. We could just get on with our business now: to improve beautify the world, to understand and be understood.

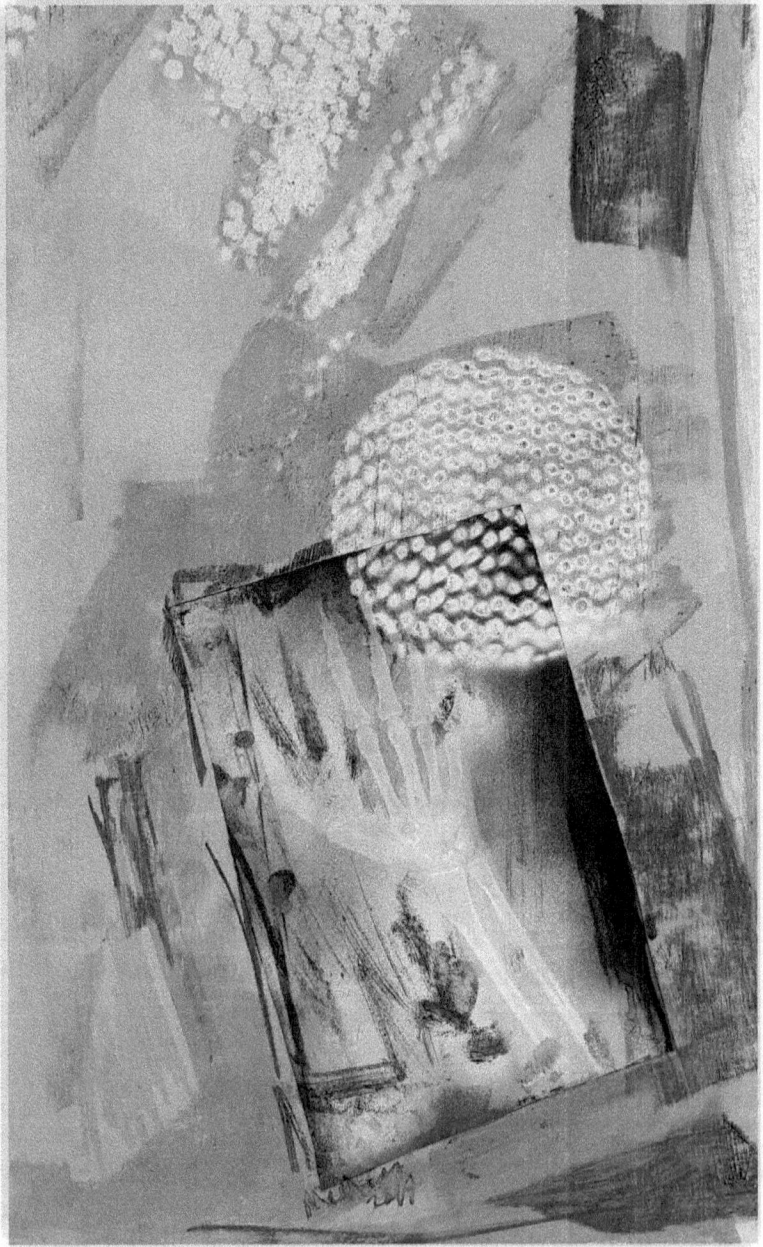

Art Picture 2: M. Söylemez "Resistance"

3 - THE CONSCIOUS AND UNCONSCIOUS BRAIN

Conscious and unconscious brain

Watch!
Two playful butterflies
One is called conscious,
The other, unconscious mind
Dance in my head aligned

Conscious mind
A soldier of the rational,
A captain passing through the gale,
To ensure the voyage does not fail,
Using logic, to keep hearty and hale

Unconscious mind,
My childlike, dreamy butterfly
Wandering in my dreams plays
Believes in fantasies but will cry
When its wishes are not complied

My butterflies!
Dance in my head in harmony
Feel the wind of love unconsciously
To hoist my sails peacefully
To heal my body silently

Science in a Nutshell

How does our brain affect our perceptions, emotions, thoughts and behavior?

The brain has long been considered the most important organ, the one at the center of our emotions, thoughts and behavior, enabling humans to comprehend the universe. Psychiatry, which overlaps with neuroscience and analyzes the effect of our emotions and thoughts on our behavior, is a relatively new (approximately 150 years) branch of science. The foundations were laid by scientists such as Sigmund Freud, Carl Jung and Carl Wernicke, and modern psychiatry was built on those foundations (1-3). After observations on their patients, Freud and Jung suggested the use of the terms consciousness and unconsciousness, which form the foundations of psychiatry. They claimed that unconsciousness is a backdrop to consciousness, where a person's behavior, passions, state of emotions, memory and thoughts take place.

The anatomical and functional borders between the conscious and unconscious have not yet been properly delineated, even by neuroscience and modern imaging systems. Despite this, there are established categories based on evolutionary, anatomical and functional classifications.

Evolutionary classification

The Triune brain is a concept that tries to explain humans in evolutionary terms. It has lost its appeal because of its sequential nature, but it is still an interesting system of classification that is worth mentioning (4). According to this concept, the brain is divided into three categories:

The reptilian (R)-Complex, which is the unconsciousness, and which is situated at the base of the brain, comprising the cerebellum and brain stem.

The paleomammalian part, which forms the middle of the brain (limbic system), which is responsible for emotions, memory, smell and some autonomic body functions that is mediated by hormones and chemicals.

The developed mammal neomammalian brain, which forms the cortex and is responsible for thoughts and higher cognitive functions.

It is accepted that each of these parts interface with the other parts.

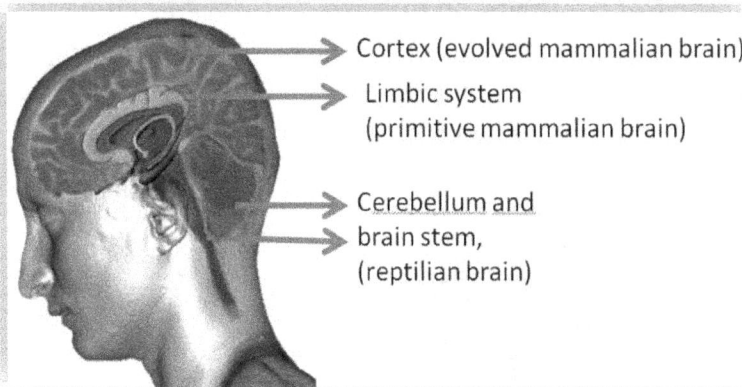

Cortex (evolved mammalian brain)
Limbic system
(primitive mammalian brain)

Cerebellum and
brain stem,
(reptilian brain)

Picture 3.1: The Triune Brain concept classifies parts of the brain in an evolutionary sequence

Anatomical classification

There is also a basic anatomical system classification that overlaps with the Triune Brain concept [Picture 3.1]. According to this system of classification, the brain stem and cerebellum, which are the parts at the base of the brain, are responsible for basic body functions such as breathing, swallowing, vision, hearing, balancing, and eye movements, all of which we do subconsciously. People whose brain stem and thalamus are damaged lose consciousness and are placed in a comatose condition.

Between the cortex, the most evolved part, and the primitive brain stem, there is the limbic system, which means "outer covering" in Latin, roughly consisting of the cingulate gyrus (emotions, character, memory), hypothalamus (which controls the body through an autonomous nervous system), amygdala (the window in the limbic system responsible for the senses), thalamus (awareness, concentration), rhinencephalon (the olfaction/smell nerve and cortex) and hippocampus (recording of memory, learning) (Picture 3.2).

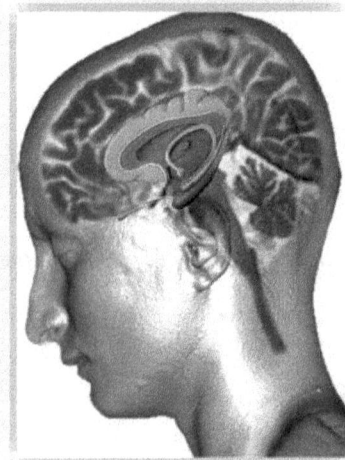

Picture 3.2. The Limbic System is located between brainstem and cortex which is illustrated in colors

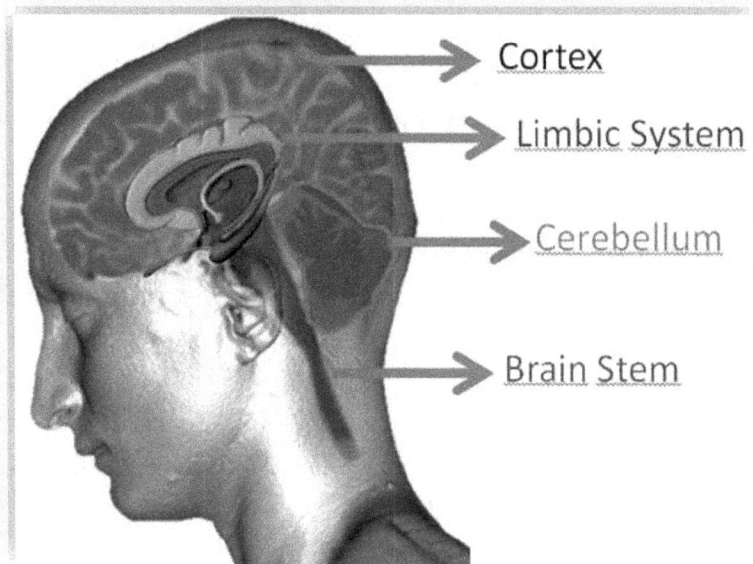

Picture 3.3: A rough classification of the brain

According to research carried out on learning and memory, the brain first and foremost learns and stores information that has intense emotional content (5). That is why the limbic system plays a big role in learning.

The limbic system is one of the main elements of the interface and border between consciousness and subconsciousness or unconciousness. It is responsible for the autonomous nervous system, which is responsible for emotions, learning, memory, and the physical reactions we display in response to our emotions. In other words, the captain's seat is situated in this part, which is responsible for controlling the body and the memories (6-9).

The hypothalamus stimulates the pineal gland in the brain to produce hormones, influenced by our thoughts and emotions, and activates the autonomous nervous system. It transmits the effects of stress and emotions to the body and the immune system. The hippocampus, which is another part of the limbic system, enables the information we learn to be stored in the memory for a long period. People whose hippocampus has been removed cannot store information in their memory for very long (10). The other parts of the brain that play a big role in consciousness or unconsciousness, memory and storage of information functions include the reticular activation systems (RAS) and thalamus. They decide which of the millions of signals should enter and be stored.

The outer shell of the brain, called the cortex, and especially the frontal lobe, is responsible for tasks such as high-level complex thoughts, decision-making, problem-solving and making plans for the future based on our experiences, deduction, memory and focus. Simply put, the parietal lobe is responsible for the senses of our sensory organs as well as body movements and calculations; the occipital lobe for vision; the temporal lobes for speech, computing what we hear, and long-term memory (11).

Functional classification

The brain can be analyzed in two categories in terms of its functions.

1-The conscious mind: This part, also called the cortex activity, forms the outer layer of the brain. Every logical mental activity and every thought that we entertain while we are awake happens in the conscious brain. Logical mental activity that conforms with social norms mostly emanates from the outer layer of the brain called the frontal lobe, which is situated just behind the forehead. We can only comprehend reality, time, and location through consciousness.

We make plans, set out objectives and do everything that is necessary to make life easy and protect the self, called the ego, using this function of the brain. The conscious mind gives orders to the subconscious mind like a ship's captain. Everything we are aware of happens in the conscious mind. It goes quiet while we are asleep. It is disciplined and regimented and acts according to a plan, like a soldier. It is responsible for short-term memory. When the cortex or consciousness is in action, for instance while learning how to ride a bike, the conscious cortex and beta waves are in control of the brain. That is why learning a new skill requires high levels of energy and some stress (12).

2- The unconscious mind: Although its sphere of activity is the entire brain, the unconscious mind mainly relates to the brain's inner part (limbic system, brain stem and cerebellum) and performs activities that are in the older parts of the brain in the evolutionary chain. The unconscious mind is the area of the brain function we are not aware of and can only be reached by special methods such as hypnosis. It completes the orders of the conscious mind without knowing or being aware of the reality. It spans the bridge between our body and the conscious mind. Long-term memory is recorded with the aid of the hippocampus (10). This has not been proven, but some psychiatrists claim that our unconscious mind starts recording when we are still in the womb, or that it can make connections, called archetypes, via the network termed the collective unconscious (13). Our faith, character, values, self-confidence, expectations in life, and habits are formed by the conscious but mostly by the unconscious. The unconscious mind is full of emotions; likes pleasure; learns through stories. That is why, during hypnosis, the practitioner will attempt to steer the unconscious by reenacting stories or providing visual representations. The more an experience or learned knowledge involves emotions, the better it is remembered and recorded in the long-term memory (5).

It is thought that the unconscious is responsible for most of the activities of the brain. The unconscious uses much less energy than the conscious mind; it can carry on an activity easily and with enjoyment (12). Once we learn how to ride a bicycle, then riding a bicycle is left to the unconscious, as though the body is on automatic pilot. A person who knows how to ride a bicycle does not emit beta waves but alpha waves, and executes the act of cycling easily, enjoying it without any stress (10,12,14). The unconscious is able, fast and creative. It works incessantly even during sleep. If we focus on a problem and try to solve it at the level of consciousness, then fall asleep, the unconscious mind continues working on it, and when we wake up we usually find the answer to the problem (12,15).

Another activity area of the unconscious is carrying out basic bodily functions, such as breathing, which we do without consciously thinking about it. We cannot stop breathing by our own will for very long. This part, which is in the brain stem, is responsible for the activities necessary for the survival of our body. If the cortex of the brain is damaged, a person can continue the functions in the brain stem in a comatose condition. However, in a comatose condition, even if the body continues its normal functions, the conscious disappears.

The conscious mind affects and controls the unconscious and the body in a series of chain reactions. Thoughts and emotions regulate automatic functions that we are not even aware of—such as sweating, feeling sick, breathing, and heart rate—all functions of the autonomous nervous system, which is part of the unconscious. For instance, a memory of feeling disgusted by a bad odor can control our body via the autonomous nervous system and cause us to vomit. Research on the links between emotions and physical health show that positive thoughts and optimism can counteract the negative effects of stress caused by the unconscious, in which the autonomous nervous system acts as an intermediary (16-18). In contrast, negative thoughts and pessimism can have a negative effect on conditions such as inflammation, body mass index, blood pressure and glucose levels by activating the stress hormones (18-21). It has been reported that the stress indicator CRP stayed high in women who had sexual trauma in their childhood even 20 years after the trauma (22). Childhood is the most sensitive period, when changes in plasticity and the immune system are occurring most rapidly.

Consequently, our brain is biologically programmed to store information accompanied by the strongest emotions and to use this information in a way that is either beneficial or detrimental to the body. Our memory does not randomly store our experiences and knowledge and then randomly lose the rest. On the contrary, it deliberately organizes and skillfully sorts out information. This process is also the engine of the ship, steering our emotions and, in turn, our physical health.

A Story and an Observation

The hidden

The throng is flowing, mingling and swirling in a torrent. As I walk down the street, my mind taking many photos of my surroundings, I become fixated on one scene in particular. Two people in their thirties, which I assume are husband and wife, are yelling at each other. The woman pulls her child towards her. The parents constantly threaten each other, not caring that there's a crowd that is watching them curiously. They continue firing threats everywhere, like bullets.

My eyes catch the sight of the 10-year-old child with them. I look into his eyes, trying to see what is going on in his mind. He is anxious, his eyes are sad; he feels embarrassed. It is apparent that he is scared. In their competition for dominance, the mother and father are using a tone of voice that evokes unpleasant memories in his eyes. No one knows what is breaking inside him, what tempests are howling, what trust is being broken. Hope and faith are drifting away. The child's sadness breaks my heart, and I can't get his sad eyes off my mind. That scenes affected me so much that I start to burst out in tears. At that very moment, an old friend suddenly stands in front of me and pulled me out my emotional sadness and deep thoughts. She asks me what is happening to me. I start to tell her the story and what I understand from that scene.

Violence and lack of love break the wings of a child and brand his heart. The blank page given him by nature becomes soiled. He becomes someone who will imitate the anger he has witnessed, who never thought to appreciate beauty, who recoils from life.

Years pass. The child grows up. He goes to a doctor and complains: "Crowds scare me. I get a lump in my throat. I break into a cold sweat in public. I get palpitations, I start breathing heavily. I feel sick, my brain freezes. All I can think of is getting away from the crowd.

The child's memory is stuck in the past, and the doctor knows this. The cause of today's panic attack is the feelings of shame and fear that have been hiding in the deepest, hidden recesses of the mind. Although his conscious mind does not remember this scene, these feelings are being triggered by the presence of a crowd. The urge to flee that spreads to his whole body is the result of conditioning; a few images stored deep in the memory are plucked from the past by the subconscious, and the conditioning that starts in the mind quickly spreads to the body.

Art Picture 3: M, Söylemez "The consciousness"

The more we heal the soul inside us, the more
developed our immune system get.
Wayne Dyer

4. THE IMMUNE SYSTEM AND THE BRAIN

My Defending Bodies

While my brain waves
Disperse into the universe,
On the wings of my thoughts and senses,
My body sings in happiness
In tune with my wellness.

Then my siblings the white blood cells,
Run into my vessel which are lanes
Deliver signals through my veins
To discharge love or stress
To heal the body and so to bless

Science in a Nutshell

What is the immune system? How does it work?

There is a defense mechanism in our body that protects us
from harmful germs and purges harmful substances that
enter our body, as well as defective and harmful cells such
as cancer cells. The immune system protects our body with
its own soldiers: the white blood cells called lymphocyte,
macrophage and leukocyte, circulating in the bloodstream.
These soldiers have a strong memory and produce
secretions similar to the hormones released by the brain. For
this reason, they can be described as tiny brains that
circulate in our blood. These soldiers can understand the
language of many tissues and cells in our body and transmit

information, as well as maintain the equilibrium of the defense system. When this sensitive equilibrium is distorted, the immune system either overworks producing allergies or autoimmune diseases, or does not work adequately, leading to our body falling prey to germs or becoming overwhelmed by defective cells such as cancer cells (1).

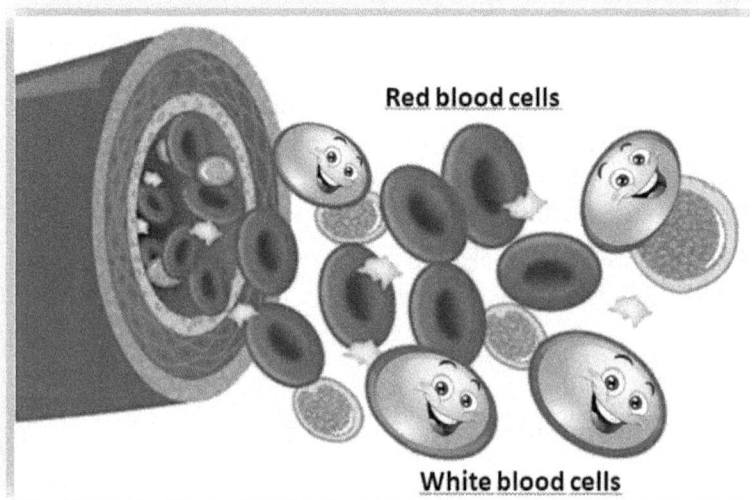

Picture 4.1: The red blood cells and the immune system cells (white blood cells) that travel in our blood.

Do our thoughts and emotions affect our immune system?

The immune system is affected by our thoughts and emotions, by way of the hypophyseal system, controlled by the hypothalamus (which is part of the limbic system, mentioned in the previous chapter) and the autonomous-adrenergic (sympathetic) system, which is connected to it (Picture 4.1). In other words, positive and negative emotions as well as stress are transmitted to all our cells by the white blood cells and hormones. In this way the immune system communicates and interacts with the other cells in the body, via what biochemistry calls neuropeptides. These hormones are released both from the nervous system and from the leukocytes (white blood cells) (2). The principal courier hormones are adrenocorticotropic hormone (ACTH), a stress hormone, corticotropin releasing factor (CRF), and endorphins (END), also known as the happiness hormone because they are released when we are happy, pleased, or during physical exercise (1,2). Apart from these, many other factors have an effect on the adrenergic system (the system which is active in conditions of stress, excitement, fight or flight) and the para-sympathetic/non-adrenergic system (engaged when we are resting, calm, and comfortable). For instance, factors such as interferon alpha, released by the white blood cells, act like adrenalin and increase the heart rate, causing excitement (3,4). As a farfetched analogy it can be said that the tiny sibling brains floating in our bloodstream are the carriers and regulators of thoughts and emotions produced in our brain.

Does stress affect our immune system?

When we feel stressed or are away from our loved ones, the stress hormones released from hypophyseal and white blood cells suppress the immune system (1). For instance, adrenalin released from the brain stem and suprarenal gland during sudden and continuous stress conditions, and cortisol released during chronic stress conditions, suppress the immune system. Because the immune system is suppressed, the healing process slows down, while the risk of cardiovascular diseases and infections increases (5).

When we are unhappy and stressed, we get sick more often and it takes longer to get better. Due to the infectious condition in our body during sickness, we lack joy and become unhappy. We quit our daily activities and shut ourselves up at home. This in itself shows that there is an intimate connection between our immune system and our emotions. The same relationship works in reverse as well.

This effect has been proved in many studies; however, there is still no full explanation as to *how* it works (6-11). This relationship raises many questions in the scientific discipline called psychoneuroimmunology. Much research has gone into trying to understand the relationship between stress and the immune system. Researchers interpret psychoneuroimmunology as being fundamentally linked to happiness.

How is the immune system suppressed?

When we are occasionally faced with danger, our emotions and thoughts activate the sympathetic system, which protects the body and transmits the message "fight or flight," taking over from the parasympathetic system, which is in command when relaxed (Picture 4.2). In a macro environment that is conducive to good health, this situation should not happen frequently, nor last long. However, in the modern age, the "fight or flight" response often turns into a chronic stress condition such as anger, anxiety and sorrow that lasts longer than expected. These feelings take charge of the body. In this situation, the stress hormone cortisol spreads to the whole body, the equilibrium of the T lymphocyte cells, which keep the immune system in balance, is distorted, and diseases start to appear. Even the memory cells in the brain start to die. There is more propensity to develop diseases such as Alzheimer's, Parkinson's and multiple sclerosis (MS) (1,2,12-14). In degenerative diseases such as Alzheimer's, it has been shown that the blood cells called lymphocytes transgress the blood-brain barrier and settle in the brain tissue.

The cancer cells that frequently occur in the body during normal cell division are usually cleared and discharged by the immune system. However, if the immune system is suppressed and consequently cannot perform its functions properly, the equilibrium between the cells gets distorted and the body cannot cope with the defective cancer cells. As a result, the cancer cells gradually grow and reach the stage where they cannot be dealt with.

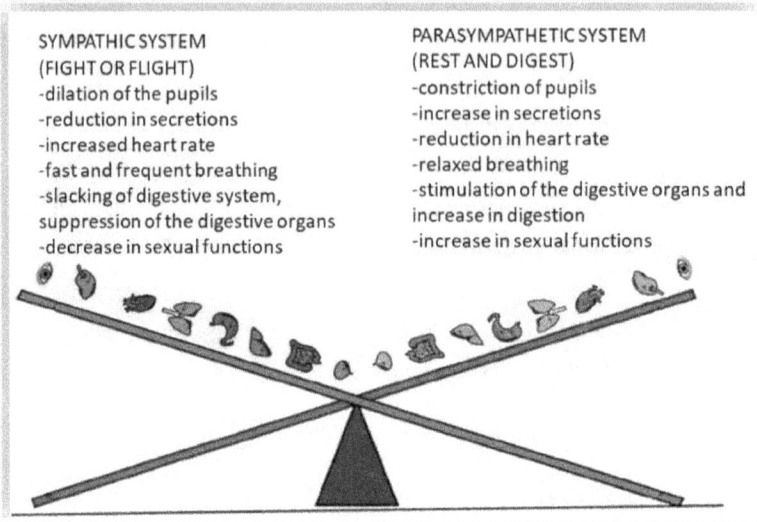

SYMPATHIC SYSTEM
(FIGHT OR FLIGHT)
-dilation of the pupils
-reduction in secretions
-increased heart rate
-fast and frequent breathing
-slacking of digestive system, suppression of the digestive organs
-decrease in sexual functions

PARASYMPATHETIC SYSTEM
(REST AND DIGEST)
-constriction of pupils
-increase in secretions
-reduction in heart rate
-relaxed breathing
-stimulation of the digestive organs and increase in digestion
-increase in sexual functions

Picture 4.2: The balance between the sympathetic system, which triggers the flight or fight response, and the parasympathetic system, which is in command during relaxation.

How can we strengthen our immune system?

The immune system can be strengthened by the activities we choose. Resting, exercise—especially yoga—tai chi, meditation, a quiet and stress-free environment, being in nature, spending time with friends and alone, positive thoughts and emotions, laughter, musical activity, and singing all boost our immune system, protect us from illness and cure us of illness (1,15-23). Moreover, studies have established that spending time in surroundings where volatile aromatic compounds released into the air by plants, called phytoncides, are abundant, for instance in a forest, helps prevent lymphocyte proteins from being activated in the body, and thus strengthens the immune system (24,25).

In summary, the link between the immune system and the nervous system, and consequently the link with our emotions and thoughts, has been well-established by clinical observations over centuries, and proved in many scientific studies. (1, 23-26). In an article published in *Nature* in 2013, it was emphasized that immunology (the scientific discipline that deals with the immune system) is an area that involves the study of happiness (26). It seems clear that one of the best methods to maintain our health and recover from illnesses is positive thinking and happiness. The reality of this link highlights time and time again the importance of a positive relationship between the patient and the physician, as well as the patient and his or her environment. It also reminds us that medicine is an art.

A Story and an Observation

The power of "now"

During a flight, while I was enjoying reading a book and sipping my tea, I also engaged in a conversation with a young woman sitting next to me. The young woman was looking after her mother, an elderly woman who was visibly unwell and in great pain, with such affection and care. I was trying to understand what was wrong with the elderly woman, who I learned was 85 years old. After living in her village for many years, she had gone to visit her daughter in the city, where she started to feel unhappy and lonely and subsequently fell ill. She wanted to go back to the village where she was born and raised. From what the daughter told me, the mother kept on saying that life in the big city was not a good lifestyle, that it merely involved working in a competitive environment, shopping and watching TV.

From what the daughter told me, I realized the hip pain that did not respond to painkillers was an autoimmune disease: one caused by the body's own immune system. The daughter asked my advice as a doctor. I told her that her mother would most probably recover if she returned to her village, friends, nature, and her "present." I touched the old woman's body and felt her pain with my hand and body. We shared, sensed and dissolved the pain together with our joined strength. The elderly woman fell asleep. That was the start of her recovery. I, deep in thought, continued reading Eckhart Tolle's book *The Power of Now*." Amid our ruthless competition to be on top, negative emotions such as anger, depression, and envy can cause illnesses, just as they did in this woman. It's a process we are unaware of, one the conscious self doesn't recognize.

The old woman who was sleeping right next to me was a living example of this reality.

Our mind constantly revisits past experiences. Most of the time it also makes us forget the present while we make plans and set targets for the future. The book continues: "To feel the moment is also to be aware of the body and the present. Neither the mind nor the ego is creative. The mind, whose only objective is making life easy, has enslaved the body and the present moment."

If you are not aware of your body, you cannot feel your emotions, and ultimately you start perceiving them as an indicator of illness at the physical level. In other words, the emotions that cannot reach out to their owner find an outlet by knocking loudly on the owner's door, using the bodily pain caused by illnesses to draw our attention. We physicians, in our turn, try to save the situation using mostly medications that have been developed in the service of a money-making machine. While the throngs gather at our door seeking treatment, we offer rote solutions, without even really touching and understand emotions of our patients. Most of the time, there is no time for customized treatments. Everything has to be speedy; everyone is in a hurry. We often assume that patients just want a prescription, or to have an X-ray taken. Amid this incessant rush, patients wander here and there in this way...

Art Picture 4: M. Söylemez "Death of a cell"

There is another I inside me.

Yunus Emre

5- DNA: OUR INTERNAL HIDDEN LIBRARY

DNA Library

Little girl
You opened your eyes in an Arcadian world
Born in a race, in a creed and in a dress for a girl
And now seek to find your own goal
Although others see your life as fate to unfurl

Her mother said in lullabies
To her wondering, innocent eyes
She will watch the earth and skies
Dough like, her body and personal mind
One day will be proud of mankind

Little girl!
While you travel through life
Don't forget the secrets that lie
In your inner hidden library nearby
Waiting to be deciphered and inscribed
To be used as your life guide

When you find the courage and when the time comes,
Handle your inner scripture with kid gloves
The one known by science,
Which can guide you with brilliance,
To find your way toward balance
And make your world a paradise.

Picture 5.1: The little girl who was the author's inspiration

Science in a Nutshell

What is DNA and the genetic symphony?

In the kernel of every cell of the human body, of which there are trillions, there is a secret library called deoxyribonucleic acid (DNA), or the genome. This library is formed of 46 shelves shaped like butterflies, called chromosomes. The books on these shelves are lined up in a spiral form that looks like the teeth of a zipper. The zipper contains pages of information, part of which come from the father and part from the mother. Each tooth of the zipper, in other words, the information on the pages, is coded by letters or notes called DNA. They are inside the protein packaging called histones. These codes—that is, the DNA zipper—link up like the poles of a magnet pulling each other and are packed together. When the zipper is in action—that is to say, when the genetic symphony is played—it opens up; at other times it is closed.

The DNA zipper teeth are tightly packed around the histones in the coded language. Each code turns into a sentence called a "gene," of which we have at least 25,000 in our body (1,2). Each gene gives a command to the body. This command is relayed from one cell to another by couriers called proteins. In this manner, the genetic symphony, composed in the body's secret library, starts to play quietly.

Picture 5.2. DNA is like a library written in molecular codes.

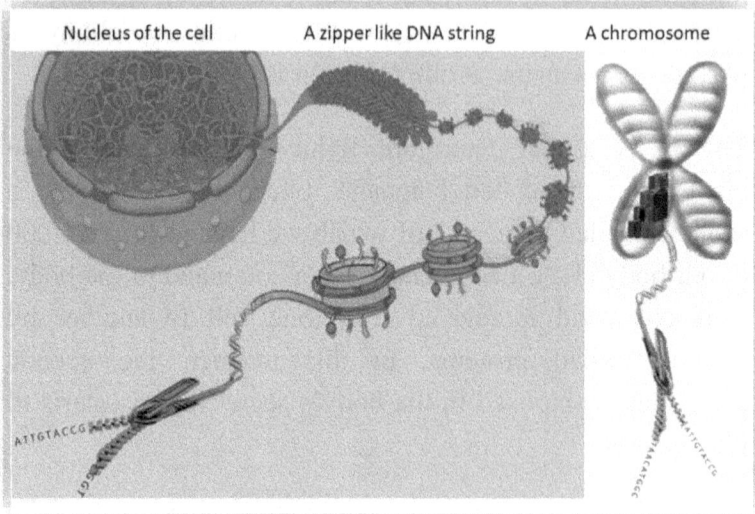

Nucleus of the cell   A zipper like DNA string   A chromosome

Picture 5.3. Each book is hidden in the nucleus of the cell. DNA library is formed of chromosomes which are shaped like a butterfly. DNA strings are lined up in a spiral form that looks like the teeth of a zipper.

How is the genetic symphony played?

Throughout our lives, conducted by our brain and executed harmoniously by the cells in our body, our DNA, or genome, is performing quietly in our bodies. There are marks, like punctuation marks in a sentence, or the notes in a sheet of music, on histones and DNA. These marks control the opening and closing of the zipper. Sometimes there is such a blockage on the zipper that it never opens. In other words, the gene is never expressed or transcribed. This blockage can even be passed onto the next generation. Sometimes these marks and notations prompt the zipper to open more frequently than usual and the gene to be expressed or transcribed more than necessary.

The genetic symphony is performed by playing the notation books stored in the DNA library. The genes in the DNA behave in a dynamic mechanism, which constantly changes in line with certain actions that science refers to asacetylation, phosphorylation, ubiquitination, simulation and methylation. These mechanisms are affected by internal and external circumstances (epigenetic). Moreover, in the process of transforming from the DNA cell into protein, the genetic symphony is further fine-tuned by another mechanism called ribonucleic acid (RNA), which functions like a writer of the sentences. The amount of protein that will be synthesized is adjusted with incredible precision (1,2). This precision is so important that, for instance, in the mother's womb, the wrong transcription of a gene at the wrong time means a disability or a disease that will last for a lifetime.

What information is stored in the DNA library?

A lot of information, such as our physical and personal characteristics, our life span, our aging process, the diseases we are inclined to develop, and our abilities are recorded in the genes, the books stored in our DNA library. Barring intervening accidents, major diseases that we will experience during our lifetime and perhaps even our cause of death are recorded in this library (2). In other words, our fate is in our DNA. This secret information, which can be deciphered by scientists with the aid of the waves in the electromagnetic spectrum, is called the *genotype*. Depending on whether they are dominant or not, the genes that come from the mother and the father present themselves as physical and biological characteristics called the *phenotype*.

In some genes, there can be changes or defects called mutations, which may be passed on from our ancestors or can occur during our lives. However, if one of the genes that comes from the mother, or the father is healthy, and the defective gene is not the dominant one, the protein synthesis necessary for the proper biological function can occur, and generally, the genetic disease does not appear or will show few symptoms. This is the reason marriage between close relatives is not recommended. In such situations, since there's an increased chance of a baby receiving defective genes from both mother and father, the risk of genetic disease rises.

Can DNA be damaged? Can the damage be reversed?

DNA can occasionally be damaged by physical and environmental stress. Chromosomes can break, have lesions, or there can be modifications, or mutations, that cause diseases and changes in the body. This damage can be passed on from one generation to the next. However, there are DNA repair mechanisms that correct the lesions in chromosomes. Thanks to these repair mechanisms, developing an illness, for instance getting cancer, is not that easy. In order to develop cancer, mutations have to accumulate and reach a stage when the damage can no longer be repaired. In addition, there are T lymphocytes in our immune system that hunt out the cancer cells. The mutant cell has to succeed in fleeing from T lymphocytes. Once it successfully escapes, the mutant cell multiplies at a very fast pace and aggressively spreads throughout the body.

Are immortality, aging and our life expectancy coded in our DNA?

Cancer cells are immortal. Immortality is caused by an enzyme called the telomerase enzyme, which prevents aging of the DNA. Aging of DNA occurs when the telomere caps at the ends of the chromosomes shorten and the DNA is filled with harmful mutations that form subsequently. However, the most important phase is the shortening of the telomeres. In fact, even our lifespan is recorded in the books called telomeres in the DNA library. Telomeres, which are at a certain length when we are born, get shorter each time a cell divides in our body. As time goes by, the DNA gets copied so many times that there comes a point when it can no longer copy itself. In other words, the cell, by giving birth to its baby, embarks on a programmed path of suicide (apoptosis) until it cannot renew itself (3). In effect, this is aging. Therefore, when telomeres fall to a critical level, our life ends. Nevertheless, there is a natural enzyme in the body that prevents the shortening of the telomeres: the telomerase enzyme. Telomerase exists in normal as well as stem and cancer cells. However, the levels in normal cells are much lower than those in stem and cancer cells. For this reason, while the rate of division in normal cells is low, in cancer cells it is infinite. In other words, the increase in telomerase is directly proportionate to the increase in cell division. The increase in telomerase in cancer cells causes an increase in cell division, while a decrease leads to the death of cancer cells. By using this relationship, scientists are working on finding medication to treat diseases like cancer.

What is the equilibrium of death and life in the genetic symphony?

In our genetic symphony, there is an equilibrium that moves backwards and forwards, like a dance, oscillating between life and death. As well as the genetic characteristics passed on from our ancestors, oxidative stress and living conditions have a decisive effect on whether the shortening of telomeres happens quickly or slowly. When telomeres run out, life ends. By the time the shortening of telomeres has reached a critical level, DNA damage has also accumulated significantly. When damaged DNA cannot be repaired, and the cell cannot multiply itself the only one option is available: programmed cell death. In other words, apoptosis, or the suicide mechanism, which is in action, perpetually enabling our lives to continue. On the other hand, the shortening of the telomeres can be reversed —that is to say, the telomere can be lengthened by alternative means, or the symphony of life can be sustained by the budding of new stem cells (4). Millions of our cells die by apoptosis every day, and new cells are formed by stem cells. In other words, there is a constant cycle in our body. Sometimes the genes that activate apoptosis in the body are suppressed, and the genes called oncogene, which activates cancer formation, become dominant. In these situations, cancer develops. There is a fine balance between proliferation and apoptosis in the cells. This balance is a good example of the fine-tuning in the genetic symphony. If the equilibrium is distorted in favour of proliferation, cancer develops; it is distorted in favour of apoptosis, autoimmune diseases develop, causing extermination of the self.

How is the genetic symphony affected by our emotions, thoughts, habits, and environmental factors?

There are genes called the *immediate early genes* in our DNA library, which are activated by our emotions and thoughts and stimulate the genes responsible for regulating our immune system (5). For this reason, positive emotions and conditioning, happiness, joy in life, a sense of purpose and positive goals, a clean environment, healthy habits including healthy diet, as well as our genetic symphony are all at the service of sustaining our body. Epigenetic modifications—genes that are modified by extrinsic and intrinsic signals—are also passed on to our children and grandchildren by a process of protein formation. The branch of science called epigenetics looks into how illnesses interact with intrinsic and extrinsic circumstances through systems such as DNA methylation, histone modification, and micro RNA (5-7). Among the environmental factors that regulate the opening and closing of the genes are stress, conditioning, nutrition, smoking and alcohol consumption habits, traumatic brain damage, and air pollution; these systems decide how the cells are affected by those environmental factors. In other words, our genetics are not fixed and certain, as if etched in stone. On the contrary, it is a dynamic system that is affected by many factors, including our own will.

This concept is supported by scientific evidence and medical observations. For instance, in many degenerative diseases such as Alzheimer's and psychiatric illnesses like schizophrenia, epigenetic factors play a big role (7-12). Chemical and hormonal signals derived from our habits, such as smoking, which happens by our own choice, as well

63

as from our emotions and thoughts, are transcribed by the hypothalamus in our brain and then transmitted sequentially, first to the hypophysis and then to the adrenal glands. These signals are recorded in every organ of the body, including the intestines, in the immune system, in the nucleus of every cell and in the body's DNA library, and are subsequently passed on to our children and grandchildren (13).

Another similar example is a protein called neurotrophin, which is controlled by the gene called Brain Derived Neurotrophic Factor (BDNF). BDNF is responsible for the protection of brain cells, as well as the renewal and curing of the nerve cells. In neurology, this is called plasticity. In stress conditions, BDNF is suppressed, causing weakening of the neurons and leading to the eventual extermination of the weak neurons. BDNF levels can be measured in blood and urine. Low levels of BDNF in serum and high levels in urine are indications of stress. BDNF levels fall during the depression and increase with treatment. It has been shown that BDNF also plays a big role in bladder and urine function disorders (1-2, 14-16).

In summary, although we have a genetic heritage inherited from our ancestors, it is not etched in stone. Thousands of pieces of information, permutations and sentences hidden in the DNA library are subject to constant modification. Every interaction among humans breeds a thought, an emotion, and consequently a neurochemical change that affects the body. It is within our power to choose and shape the kind of interactions we have with the environment. Emotions and thoughts, as well as past experiences, the choices we make, and our perceptions of our inner world—all pick messages from this genetic library. Regardless of whether the emotions and thoughts are real or imaginary, the body applies the content of the message.

We, as humans, are the only living beings who have the ability to change our genetic symphony and fate through our choices and awareness. For this reason, we have to be aware of the power of our own consciousness and apply this power to make life a better place for, first, ourselves, then for other living beings.

A Story and an Observation

The house that hasn't lost its goats

One day I fancy some natural goat's milk. The branded products sold in grocery shops do not interest me. I quietly follow the shepherd who grazes his goats in the empty field behind my house.

The shepherd in the front, the goats in the middle, and I, at the back, follow the same path, away from my neighborhood and into a suburban ghetto of the kind that's frequented by police vehicles and ambulances.

The neighborhood and the children on the street are unkempt. There are no trees, no sidewalks along the dusty roads, yet the streets are full of women and children curious about me. The children gather around and ask what I am looking for. Since I've now lost track of the shepherd, I ask these smart and daring children where his house is.

"You mean Siddik's house? Siddik with the disabled children and goats? He's the only one with goats in this area."

The children and I troop together into a shabby street and stop in front of an unpainted house with a rusty iron door and iron bars on the windows. There is a woman, presumably Siddik's wife, on the roof of the house. I ask the woman on the roof, who is wearing a muslin headscarf, "Do you have goat's milk?"

The woman replies, "No."

I ask, "When would you have some? What is your name?" Looking towards a window of the house, I continue, "What's wrong with these children?"

The children I am referring to are the two girls and a boy with curly hair, all of them with crossed big curious dark eyes, who are watching me from the window, behind iron bars, as in a prison, with open mouths. The girls have linked arms and they're clustered close together, trying to communicate to me with their big smiles.

My disappointment about the no-milk reply must have shown on my face, for now, one of the girls, who looks about 15, appears before me with a bottle of milk in her hand. She is trying to please me with her good manners and pure heart, despite the disability that renders her unable to speak.

I show the bottle of milk to the mother on the roof and ask, "Didn't you say there was no milk?" The daughters grin cunningly, as if taking revenge on their mother.

"Would one kilo be enough?" asks the mother on the roof.

"It's enough! It's enough!" I reply, satisfied at having achieved my objective.

I cannot resist asking, "All three of the children are disabled. Are you a relative of your husband?"

The woman answers from the roof, "Our mothers are sisters."

"Hmm, I see," I reply. I wonder whether the disabled girl's anger aimed at her mother was because she had violated the laws of nature.

I remember the words of my lecturer at university: "Marriage between close relatives means crippled humans."

Nature becomes most beautiful with variety: variety brings ability, perfection and beauty. The genetic codes take revenge on those who do not contribute to this variety. Marriage between close relatives, making a choice against nature that ignorance calls "fate" or "custom," can turn life into a misery. Despite this, nature cannot help adding, even in her products some might call "defective," the virtues of purity, kindness and generosity that are intrinsically present in all unadulterated living beings.

It also teaches a lesson to the politicians who propagate pure race as a policy, by implying that the more you mix, the better you get.

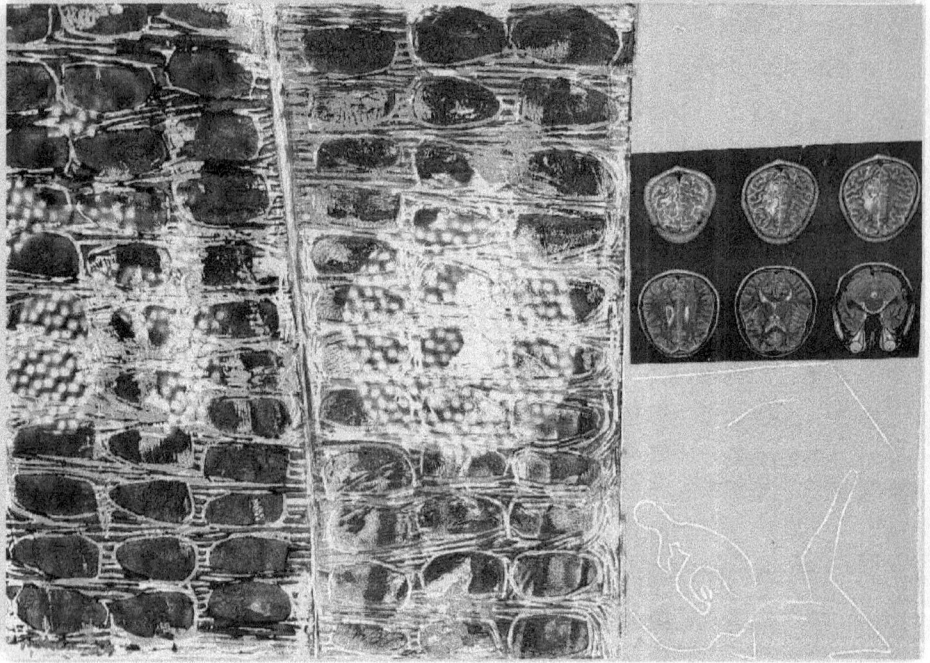

Art Picture 5: M. Söylemez "DNA Library"

There is no illness without a cure, other than lack of will.
There is no worthless plant,
other than the lack of being recognized.
Ibn-i Sina [Avicenna]

6 - BELIEVING IN THE CURE: CURING BY PLACEBO

Placebo

If I can find the lost key
I am looking for to see
Under the light of the science's tree
Then I am carefree

If I can't find my lost key
Under the light of the science's tree
Take the medicine placebo as a strategy
Which science supports and agrees
When I believe a placebo is the remedy

Science in a Nutshell

What is a placebo? How effective is it in curing illness?

Scientists working on medical drug trials give one group of people the newly invented medication, while another group is merely given a placebo, typically composed of sugar, water or oil, which is not a drug. People take this placebo thinking it is medication. If they believe they will be cured, in other words if they are conditioned to believe it will work, they may be "cured," depending on the illness, at a rate between 10% and 100% (1,2). For instance, with a placebo that mimics a painkiller but has none of the chemicals that stop pain, half of the people given it find relief from a headache or complaints related to irritable bowel syndrome (3,4). Also, in a wide-ranging study carried out on cancer patients in 2017, it was shown that the painkiller paracetamol, which is widely used in hospitals, had no different effect than a placebo (5,6).

Similar findings were reported for symptoms such as vomiting, depression, asthma, Parkinson's, attention deficit disorder, migraine and headaches (7,13). These studies showed that a placebo affected the brain's signaling pathways by steric and biochemical mechanisms, just like the real drugs (13). For instance, it was shown that in Parkinson's disease, which is caused by a disorder in the dopamine mechanism, a placebo had the effect of increasing the release of dopamine. However, the success rate of achieving results by placebo was very low in schizophrenia, obsessive compulsive disorder and dementia (7,8).

In which illnesses is a placebo effective?

It has been established that a placebo works in mild emotional disorders such as panic attacks and depression. While the drugs used to treat panic attacks are effective at a rate of 50% to 60%, a placebo has been found to be 50% effective. The success rate of treating depression with drugs is 50%–60%, while a placebo is 30%–40% effective. In some studies, the success rate of treatment with a placebo exceeded that of antidepressants (14,16).

In another study, it was observed that 25% of patients suffering from high blood pressure benefited from a placebo. Allergic rhinitis patients benefited at a rate of 50%–75%. Also, placebo injections are found to erase the symptoms of itchiness. While the rate of recovery by placebo in stomach ulcers is approximately 40%, this rate differs in various studies, between 0% and 100%. Moreover, nearly half of patients suffering from thinning hair, insomnia, sexual disorders and hot flushes benefited from a placebo. Even in advanced-stage cancers, a 3% reduction in the size of tumors as well as a 10% reduction in the symptoms were recorded. All these studies indicate that placebo is effective, especially in stress-related immune system illnesses. However, placebo is not as effective in chronic diseases. It should be noted that placebo is not recommended in bacterial infections, cancers that can be cured by surgery and drugs, or in fractures. In other words, depending on the conditioning of the patient, placebo usually works in mild psychosomatic illnesses (common cold, mild traumas, etc.). It has been proven that a placebo can be effective even if the patient knows it is a placebo. The changes caused by a placebo were also proved by functional MRI. It is noteworthy that this effect is more pronounced in children (2, 7, 18).

How accepted is a placebo and how is it used in treatments?

Thanks to the clinical observations mentioned above, since the second half of the 20th century, placebo has been an integral part of pharmaceutical studies (randomized controlled trials, and placebo control studies). The U.S. National Institutes of Health held a wide-ranging, multi-disciplinary conference to discuss "placebo in science," with the participation of hundreds of researchers. It was decided after this conference to support studies on placebo and its clinical applications. Treatment by placebo as an ethical treatment for certain illnesses was entered in the treatment guidance in 2007 by the American Medical Association (7). Harvard professor Thomas Delbanco (1994) especially recommended placebo to patients suffering from depression, an old-fashioned, effective, simple, easy and mysterious treatment as an alternative to the current treatments involving advanced technology (18).

How does placebo cure?

Curing by placebo, or recovering by the power of our own body, guided by our belief that healing may be fueled by our own internal resources (2,7,18,19), is free, easy and harmless. After receiving the "you can be cured" command and conditioning received from the conscious mind, the unconscious mind and body set to work. When the unconscious makes the decision to cure and cling to vitality, it focuses on beauty and kindness. Thinking of healing in storylines stimulates the unconscious and the body to take steps toward healing. Attention and awareness must focus only on healing, longevity, kindness and happiness. In this process, conditioning, the autonomous nervous system, and the unconscious mind play the most important roles (2). Moreover, the trust between the patient and the physician is one of the most important factors in healing with a placebo.

In stark contrast to this, expecting a negative prognosis or negative outcome from treatment, complaining and dwelling on worst-case scenarios has a detrimental effect. This adverse effect is called *nocebo*, a Latin word (2, 20). Panic, anxiety, and focusing on undesirable outcomes during crises and illness delay recovery. For this reason, the conscious should constantly focus on recovery. It's important to convey the desired outcome to the unconscious, which requires creativity: stories, positive thoughts, and meditation.

In summary, placebo is an internal intelligence and power that constantly feeds life. Science has only recently started to understand the biology of belief. The belief referred to here is not about traditional religious belief. It's about belief in the wellness and power of humans; belief in healing, in being in unity with the universe, as well as belief in hope, in perfection and beauty of life and nature.

A Story and an Observation

A typical placebo story from Anatolia/Asia Minor

Many years ago, in a village in southeastern Turkey, which used to be called Kefer Havar, a village of Midyat, Mardin, notable for being one of those places where various religions and cultures lived together harmoniously, there was a hodja called Sheikh Omer. He was renowned for his wit and understanding. Rumor had it that anyone who made a wish and slept for one night in the yard of the shrine where one of Sheikh Omer's ancestors was buried would get their wish; the deranged would be rid of their madness in one night. Sacrifices and vows were made. Every night the shrine would be filled with people looking for a cure.

One day a Yazidi woman called Yezida turned up with acorns and a wicker basket full of firewood and stood in front of Sheikh Omer. After offering her gifts, she told him her grievance. Despite trying for many years, Yezida could not bear children. Her husband was threatening to leave her for another woman.

According to myth, Yazidis call the cabbage "our mother" and regard Angel Tavus, which is sometimes known as Satan by other religions, as holy and blessed. Their heretical views and attitudes made them the butt of children's jokes in the neighborhood. Yet they lived in harmony with Muslims and Christians in the village for many centuries.

"O Sheikh Omer, you are reputed for being formidably effective in helping people, do help me as well!" she pleaded with the Sheikh. She wished for a son from God. Sheikh Omer thought for a long time and decided that a talisman prepared for Muslims would not be appropriate for Yezida. He wrapped up a piece of goat's droppings in a triangular shape to emulate a talisman and gave it to Yezida. She returned to her village feeling exuberant.

After a year, Yezida came to visit Sheikh Omer with a healthy baby boy and a goat kid as a gift. She offered the kid along with the acorns to the Sheikh, to show her gratitude. She told her story to everyone. The fame of the shrine and the talismans was passed on from generation to generation.

Upon hearing the story, a physician remarked, "a typical placebo story." She started writing a typical placebo-curing story, whereby the people of Anatolia produced healing in their own body and mind, all the while thinking it was someone else's doing.

Art Picture 6: M. Söylemez "Hope, placebo"

7 - STRESS AND THE AUTONOMIC NERVOUS SYSTEM

Stress

The pollution of our generation
The plague of our century
More vigorous than a bacillus
Leaves us helpless,
Induces illness,
Wrecks the body.
This heavy load:
What should I do with you?

'I have an idea,' said human brain
Let's find a way to drain
Imagine a cruise to entertain
Takes you on an Aegean Sea lane
A way to find relief from this strain,
Use meditation to feel light and unchained

The body replied:
'I like this way of play.
When I listen to what my breaths say
I feel the stress fade away,
My mind anchors in a peaceful bay
Enlightens my body in a calm way.

Science in a Nutshell

What is stress?

Stress can be defined as any stimulant that alters the physiological equilibrium, also called homeostasis, caused by either innate or external sources. This subject has been studied in its many facets by scientists. The renowned neuroscientist Eagleman described it as the most dangerous pollutant of civilization (1). It is also possible to describe stress as the biological tissues' reaction to a real or perceived threat, as a result of which the balance of homeostasis is distorted.

Which situations cause stress?

Stress factors can be classified in many ways, based on their duration, degree of severity, and impact on the body. According to one method of classification, there are three types of stress: positive, tolerated, and toxic. Positive stress is the type that creates excitement and motivation, leading to development. The stress that can be tolerated is the kind we face in our daily lives, which we can overcome by ourselves or with the help of those around us. Toxic stress lasts longer and cannot be easily relieved, causing our body and equilibrium to be adversely affected.

In this situation, homeostasis is distorted, sending our body into a condition called allostasis (2,3). Stress can be caused by physiological factors (insomnia, exhaustion, dehydration, hunger, illness causing fever, menstrual cycle, hyperventilation), pharmacological factors (chemotherapy drugs and other medications), environmental factors (extreme hot or cold, noise, light, odor) or psychological elements (depression, anxiety, fear, anger, unhappiness, grief, etc.). Oppressive and controlling social relationships in conservative societies, high expectations that we cannot meet in the workplace, tasks we must do unwillingly, and a lack of motivation are all situations that cause us stress. In direct proportion to the severity and duration of the stress-causing factor, all these situations can alter our natural balance, causing illnesses and abnormal symptoms in our body.

Hormonal change is another example of cyclical stress. During the menstrual period, towards the end of the menstrual cycle, and just before menstruation, many women are affected by intense stimulation and stress. During this period the estrogen hormone is very dominant and the effect of progesterone, which balances the excess estrogen, can be very low by aging. Generally, estrogen has the effect of stimulating neurons, that is nerve cells, increasing the neuron metabolism. A surge of estrogen in the body increases stimulation of the neurons. Women suffering from such effects lose their temper easily and become overstimulated. It has been shown that the frequency of migraine attacks and epileptic seizures also increases during this estrogen surge. The interesting finding is that, while synthetic progestin was found to be ineffective during this period, natural micronized progesterone can regulate the overstimulation (4,5).

How does our body react to stress?

When we are faced with stress, sympathetic activity increases and parasympathetic activity, which relaxes and balances us, decreases in the autonomic nervous system.

78

We feel nervous and tense. Our blood pressure rises. We take frequent and shallow breaths. We eat and smoke more than usual. We forget about regular physical activity, sleep less, and after a while suffer from circadian rhythm disorder. Inadequate sleep causes circadian rhythm disorder, weight gain and high blood pressure. (See Picture 4.2 in chapter 4 sympathetic and parasympathetic activity)

In acute stress conditions, all energy sources in the body are mobilized, releasing the temporary hormones for fight and flight. The portions of the brain called the hypothalamus and pituitary are stimulated to send chemical and hormonal signals to the brain stem and adrenal glands. Two of the most significant hormones in such conditions are adrenalin and cortisol (6). Adrenalin is mostly associated with short-term stress, and cortisol with long-term stress. If overstimulation of the sympathetic system lasts for an extended period, it causes chronic stress.

What happens in the brain during stress?

The brain conducts the entire body by means of the neuroendocrine, autonomic and immune systems. During chronic stress conditions, it is the limbic system that gets affected first: our emotions are unstable, and we become prone to depression. Also, by causing constant stimulation and alarm in the body, stress produces adverse changes and even causes damage in our body and brain, in particular in the region relevant to processing memory, the hypothalamus (the portion of the brain that is responsible for hormones and the suprachiasmatic nucleus, which regulates the circadian rhythms) and hippocampus (6,7).

Negative stimulation of our circadian clock—that is to say, the suprachiasmatic nucleus, which works with the hypothalamus—due to stress causes the body to be adversely affected by neuronal, hormonal (cortisol, melatonin) and biochemical processes. We may begin sleeping less (under four to six hours). In connection with this, activity is reduced in the parasympathetic system, which normally balances the activity of the sympathetic system and helps us relax. More cortisol and insulin are released, leading us to feel hungrier. Some substances such as leptin, which protects us from illnesses, decrease (8). There is also a rise in the illness-causing biochemicals called cytokines, which initiate inflammation. Our psychomotor health is adversely affected. We become prone to depression, making mistakes, and gaining weight. It has been established that the presence of high levels of adrenalin in the blood for extended periods trigger disorders of the cardiovascular and immune systems, psychiatric illnesses, and cancer (7,8).

How can we overcome stress?

It is possible to overcome stress with positive feelings and activities, such as mild to moderate exercise, being alone in nature, gardening activity, meditation, laughter, love and music. Positive feelings cause the release of happiness hormones and many beneficial neurochemicals, such as endorphins, serotonin, dopamine and oxytocin. The happiness hormones protect our body by stimulating the immune system in a positive way. It has been established that yoga, meditation, exercise, nature, and music have positive effects on the immune system, as well as on lowering obesity and the risk of cardiovascular diseases (10-12).

Scientific studies and experiments have shown that happiness and stress are mostly related to social status and whether we experience high-quality relationships with other people (13). Feelings of loneliness and social isolation create stress that directly affects our genes and immune system (14). Pursuing a meaningful life is also one of the factors that reduce stress (15). Moreover, some studies show that horticultural activity reduces stress, while urban lifestyles increase the symptoms of stress (16).

How is stress linked to daily life?

Gleaned from my personal life and medical observations, a person's daily activity can be described in four stages based on general stress, anxiety and human affections.

Stage 1: This is the phase when a person is sleeping or in deep meditation. Low-frequency wave (alpha, theta, delta) activity is prevalent in the brain. The body is in a state of regeneration, healing and deep relaxation. It is a stage when creativity and intuition are strong.

Stage 2: This is when a person is awake and alert, is in a familiar and safe environment, is feeling pleased, happy, comfortable, productive and stress-free (slow beta activity). The person is productive and can learn easily. The body systems and repair mechanisms work at an optimum level.

Stage 3: In this phase, stress levels are increased, and the person is in a worrisome and unsafe environment. Fast beta activity is prevalent in the brain. Ordinarily a person switches between stage 2 and 3 in their daily life. As anxiety levels increase, the body suffers from stress symptoms such as general muscle tension and exhaustion, increased heart rate and rapid breathing. In short, overstimulation of the sympathetic system is prominent feature. If the conditions described in this stage become chronic or last for an extended period, the person advances to stage 4.

Stage 4: Long-term and chronic stress put the person in severe depression and burnout syndrome. The individual becomes apathetic, in other words incapable of showing emotions and reactions. In this condition it is noted that people sometimes lose their will to live, lose their energy and lose their joy in life. Once in this stage, it is difficult to reverse its effects and it takes time to recover from it.

In summary, even though stress is damaging to the body when suffered at high levels and for extended periods, in reality it is difficult to live a stress-free life. Moreover, having no stimulant renders life boring, as well as making it devoid of success and development. Meanwhile, when the level of stress and its effects on our body reach the limit, it is possible, with mind and body awareness, to be more proactive about protecting our health with methods such as meditation, physical exercise, engaging in enjoyable activities, being active generally, and making conscious efforts to alter our perceptions and, as much as possible, our environment (17). We have to be conscious of the fact that we are capable of making choices and changing ourselves in order to protect ourselves from stress. Taking a break is the best thing one can do when there is no time to take a break.

Negative thoughts are adverse stress factors, and sometimes these thoughts circulate in the conscious in a vicious circle, which can release unhappiness-inducing chemicals that cause continual damage to the body (18-19). In mild cases, instead of ruminating over our problems, we can resort to writing or talking to a trusted, unbiased person in order to re-channel the flow of negative thoughts; to unload the unconscious by using free association. In cases of severe depression and burnout, expert medical help should be sought from psychiatrists. The helm of the ship should be temporarily left to another trusted team or person until the brain biochemistry recuperates.

A Story and an Observation

Stress and viewpoint

Two disabled children behind the iron bars of a window in one of the houses in a ghetto are wistfully watching other children play freely in the street with much shouting and screaming. The ball bounces joyfully from one child to another. The road is narrow; cars drive by, leaving a plume of dust behind. The children don't care; they let out screams of joy…

Another child passing by the house catches a glimpse of the disabled children watching life on the street at a distance, from behind the bars, who have to stay imprisoned indoors. The child feels sorry and outraged. He wants to understand: Why keep them indoors? Is it poverty, fear, or lack of affection? Why are these children imprisoned? The boy demands the answers to these questions from his mother.

With tears welling in his eyes, the boy describes the scene that was imprinted in his consciousness since he saw it.

The mother smiles. "First, compose yourself," she says. "Why are you judging them from your own world? Those children in the ghetto who are watching the world wistfully from behind the bars are doing exactly what you are doing. Think about it: Is it those inside or outside who are locked up? Is imprisonment about being kept indoors? Or is it being locked in the dark cell of your thoughts, sentenced to do things you don't want to do? Also, don't forget, every adverse situation provides fuel for forward motion. The strongest people are those who have suffered hardship."

The mother switches on the television. A physician on a health program gives the following advice to those who phone in to complain about stress caused by others and the illnesses they suffer as a result: "Stress is entirely about your conceptions and the way you perceive matters. Other people, whom you think you have to compete with, or a situation that you don't like, can cause stress. When you disconnect the link between yourself and the competitive streak, as well as your dependency on these people, stress and anxiety are eliminated. Don't forget, it's also possible to relieve stress and anxiety by merely changing your point of view. None other than yourself can do that. Cut off your ties with those who distress you; strengthen your ties with the joy of life. Never forget that somewhere in the world there are always those who suffer more than you do. Instead of pitying yourself, feel your innate happiness and strength. Leave the environment that distresses you for a while; escape to your imagined world, however briefly it might be;

relax your body and mind with your breathing. Imagine orange groves, with children and birds playing about. Think of the red hues of the sun, or the sea waves rolling with the whispers of the universal symphony, the common language of all living beings."

Art Picture 7: M. Söylemez "Stress"

"Panic is a rearing fear; fear itself causes more damage than the feared."
Marie Curie

8 - FEAR, THE BRAIN AND THE BODY

Crude Human

Immature human with crude manner
Why are you so frightened?
Haven't they taught you how to love?
How to care for those more fragile?
Did no affectionate, sensitive tutor
Ever hold to your beautiful soul a mirror?
Didn't a wise mother, father or mentor,
Ever show you the beauty of the world,
Or teach you with humor?
Tell you what would flourish in your mind's arbor?

Is the result that
You are afraid of looking at yourself?
Is that why you act with envy and with fury?
And you strive uncontrollably
To prove yourself endlessly?

Calm down, puerile human!
Return to your inherent beauty,
Rest in your own self, sturdy
Like a wise old tree.

Don't listen to the voice of the brutal;
Fearful words can only be futile.
Let the tenets of love
Connect you to nature and all above,
To the light of life,
And the story of the whole

As an invisible cord
Binds us to the infinite soul.

Science in a Nutshell

What is fear?

Fear is a feeling induced by perceived danger. Although it is one of the factors that cause stress, its significance makes it stand out from the rest, hence the separate chapter dedicated to it.

Although fear is fundamental to survival, it can also damage the structure of the body if, as explained in the previous chapter, the fight-or-flight response shakes the foundations of life, or it is the kind of fear where traumatic long-term effects take over the mind (1-4). As with stress, this atypical condition, which takes over the body when we do not feel safe, can be tolerated for a short period. However, if fear lasts for an extended period or turns into chronic anxiety, it distorts our brain's and body's regeneration, as well as the plasticity mechanisms, by initially affecting the immune system.

How is fear felt?

Researchers in psychoanalysis emphasize that in the brain, anxiety shows itself, not in the conscious, but during imagining or reflecting (5). Sensing fear by the conscious or unconscious stimulates the amygdala part of the limbic system via the thalamic and cortico-thalamic circuits, which are stimulated along with the amygdala, and the central nucleus affects the cortices (the anterior cingulate cortex, ventromedial prefrontal cortex and orbital prefrontal cortex, which are also part of the limbic system). On the other hand, it enables the release of adrenalin and cortisol through the hypothlamo-hypophyseal axis, which prompts the flight-or-fight response to take control over the body, as was explained in the Stress and Autonomic Nervous System section in chapter 8. In certain cases, the person's biological mechanism can be suppressed, and the person becomes unable to move (6). The sympathetic system is activated when we feel fear, causing our pupils to dilate, heartbeat to speed up, blood pressure to rise, and muscles to contract. We become ready to run faster. On the other hand, organs regulated by parasympathetic activity and which are not vital for the moment, such as the digestive system, are suppressed. We lose our appetite and our intestinal movements slow down. We act with our instincts, as opposed to our logical thinking. If the fear goes to extremes, there is an increased propensity to interpret events adversely. There is a surge of blood in the hippocampus and amygdala, the parts of the brain responsible for memory and emotions. Our experience gets recorded in our memory. Almost all of the details are recorded in our brain in minute detail and remain for a long period. These memories are not forgotten easily. Even if the conditions that caused fear in the first place are eliminated, triggers such as scent, voice, or facial expression that remind us of the moment of fear can instantly prompt recollection of the scene of fear, sparking the same emotions. In other words, the slightest hint can put the person in the same panic situation. Even if our conscious suppresses the fears we experienced long ago, the information stored in our unconscious—that is, our dreams and recollections—can sometimes relay them to our conscious.

How does fear affect the brain?

The hippocampus, which acts as a bridge between the amygdala and prefrontal cortex, contains receptors sensitive to stress hormones, such as adrenalin (which plays an important role in the fight-or-flight response by increasing blood flow to muscles, output of the heart, pupil dilation and blood sugar), and stress-related hormones, such as insulin (regulates the metabolism of carbohydrates, fats and protein), leptin (helps to regulate energy balance by inhibiting hunger), ghrelin (hunger hormone) and insulin-like growth hormone factor 1 (IGF-1) (6,7). While the volume of the hippocampus, which is linked to memory, decreases in people who have experienced fear and intense stress, the volume of the amygdala, which is linked to fear and aggression (8), increases. Studies have shown that cortisol and adrenalin, the hormones released during fear and stress conditions, cause a shrinkage in the volume of the hippocampus in post-traumatic stress disorders and extended toxic stress (8).

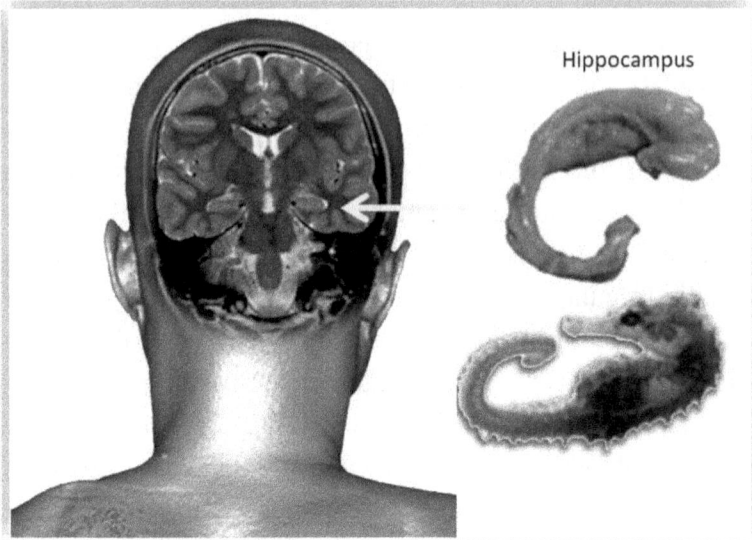

Picture 8.1: The MR imaging (left) of the limbic system's hippocampus, which is responsible for memory, and a real tissue sample (top right). An image of a seahorse (bottom right), which is what hippocampus (seahorse in Latin) looks like.

Which illnesses does fear cause?

If the event that inflicts fear is sudden, serious and has long-lasting effects (earthquake, accident, war, rape, etc.) it may cause a psychiatric condition called post-traumatic stress disorder (PTSD), which affects 9%–14 % of society (3,4). Moreover, when it lasts for long or extended periods, stress can cause many psychiatric and physical illnesses, as explained in the previous chapter.

When fear lasts for a long period, the body releases the inflammation-causing chemicals called cytosine, which precipitates chronic inflammation disorders (9,10). Our cardiovascular system suffers damage. This leads to stomach ulcers and lower intestinal diseases, such as irritable bowel syndrome. Fertility and ability to procreate decrease. By causing epigenetic damage in our DNA, it can also be passed on the next generations (11). The effects of trauma can be seen in the DNA even four months after the trauma (12,13). It has been shown that more than 25 genes in our DNA are affected by extreme fear and post-traumatic stress disorder (14). This influence starts in the DNA and has more significance for physical health, especially during the early stages of life. In particular the corticotropin-releasing hormone, which is released from the hypothalamus, can even affect the reorganization of neurons in the brain. Intense fear and trauma suffered in childhood are important causes of depression in following years (15,16). While mild fear and stress facilitate the stimulation of neurons, intense fear suppresses the neuronal cells; loss of neuron cells occurs via stress hormones and amino acids. This causes a decrease in our ability to think and after a while results in unhappiness, chronic exhaustion, and depression.

In summary, using similar mechanisms explained in the chapter on stress, fear causes significant structural changes in the brain, body, and DNA, via the autonomic nervous system and stress hormones. Overcoming stress is one of the most important stages in the treatment of chronic and psychiatric illnesses. On the one hand, to overcome fear, medical and psychiatric guidance and drug treatment are used. On the other hand, treatment methods such as meditation, music, nature therapy and physical exercise are used to help patients recover from stress.

A Story and an Observation

A Tale of the Audacious in the skies and the Audacious on the ground

Zafer the pilot takes off from a seaside city, soaring into the skies like a bird. While the red glow of the rising sun washes the mountains in pink light, the plane leaves behind the city trapped in densely packed, high-rise concrete blocks.

Shortly after reaching the outskirts of the city, mountains come into view… glorious dark-green mountains, covered with pine forests. It is autumn. Dirt roads, lakes and brooks flow down from the peaks. When viewed from above, Anatolia becomes a mysterious, enchanted painting.

Zafer the pilot gets excited again. His brave heart is overwhelmed by the magic of beauty. Suddenly, his eye catches red patches that stretch towards the foothills. They look like vineyards. Next to them is a small cottage with a red-brick roof and a smoking chimney.

He leaves the mountains and villages behind. But the image of the small cottage lingers in Zafer's mind.

While his plane hops from one city to another, the pilot's eyes always search for that single cottage. He wonders which crazy hermit lives in it. One weekend, he decides to drive over the mountains to find that little cottage, but more importantly to find the one who dwells in it.

On Sunday morning he sets off, on his own, with some cheese and sesame bagels. He drives through villages and hamlets on long, winding roads. He passes by pomegranate groves, vineyards, lambs, and cattle on his way off the beaten track. Eventually he reaches the vineyards.

The joyous chirping of birds guides him towards the remote cottage, and he finds himself standing in front of the little door. Smoke is coming out of the chimney like a veil wafting in a gentle breeze.

He calls out, "Is anybody there?"

A kitten dozing in front of the door opens her eyes and, taking no notice of him, continues to doze. A portrait of Ataturk hanging in the window winks at the pilot.

A dog runs towards him, leaping and bounding. He lets out yelps and barks, more out of excitement than to inspire fear. He rubs himself against the pilot's legs; stretches his neck up, pleading for the pilot's attention and affection.

All of a sudden, the door is opened half-ajar. An old man wearing a thick woolen cardigan steps out. "Are you looking for something? Who are you? What is it that you want?" he asks.

The pilot tells him why he came, how he was curious about this cottage and wanted to meet its resident.

The old man introduces himself. "I'm Tahsin. Since you came for me, you are my guest sent by God. Come on in. The range is on, the tea is already brewing."

Zafer the pilot is not surprised at this. He brings out the bag with the cheese and sesame bagels. He makes himself comfortable next to the range, whispering, "Just what I needed!" He gazes at the grapes outside, which are redder than the autumn leaves. They start to talk.

Uncle Tahsin asks the young man, "What do you do for a living?" Zafer replies, "You know those planes that fly above those peaks?" He points towards the mountains. "I'm a pilot flying one of those planes."

Uncle Tahsin looks surprised. He asks, "Aren't you scared of crashing from such heights?" Zafer replies, "What about you? Aren't you scared of living on your own in such a remote area? Tell me, how old are you?"

The old man Tahsin smiles. "I must be well over one hundred. I planted these vineyards. I toiled for many years to bring the redness of the grapes to the redness of the soil. The vines, the quince trees, the leaping dog, they are all like my children. I am not scared of anyone other than God, and I've never needed to go to a hospital. I drink the water from the well and eat the grapes from my vines; these cure me even if I am sick. I cannot be a servant to another man slavishly. I refuse to be imprisoned in a city. I am not scared of getting ill and will not, cannot run. The Grim Reaper has never visited me in my hundred-odd years. He roams around those who worry about their impending death. Or those who are afraid of losing their body and material possessions.

"The beauty of these mountains is enough for me, the eggs of my hens, the homemade bread, water in my well, my birds.

"Breathe in some fresh air while I get some peppers from the garden. Have them with your bagel. You'll remember it when you fly from above."

The talk went on. The pilot used to think he was brave until he listened to the fearless wisdom of Uncle Tahsin, accumulated for over a hundred years. He ruminated over this pleasant encounter, as if he was living in a dreamland, while he chewed his bagel.

Art Picture 8: M. Söylemez "Disintegration"

In life, two things are important for everything:
being able to inhale and exhale.
G. Bruno

9 - RESPIRATION

Where the blue sea and sky meet, the sun rolls over to the other side of the earth with a glorious display of shades of red. People who are watching the red hues of the sun and the waves unwittingly feel drawn into romanticism. They stop their darting about, even their chattering. The "life energy" released into the air by thoughts joins the sound of the waves and the waves created in the air. In eastern cultures this is called *prana*, and it comprises all cosmic energy, permeating the universe at all levels.

It is absorbed through the pores into the bodies of those who are silently watching the harmonious display of the sky, the sea and the horizon. Oxygen, the fuel used by everyone, drifts towards the lungs. While all the cells are intoxicated with the source of life, while all toxins are released towards the green leaves of a tree, the human body is regenerated, healed and energized with this breath...

Swinging between life and death
My subconscious is a curtain-like net
Swaying, at every breath,
Between the soul and the conscious at rest.

When I watch my breathing mindfully
Flurry and fears fade away, silently;
Then my thoughts become carefree.

Oh, my dearest breath!
Let's swing between life and death.
My serene voice of curing faith
Increase the glow of my inner light
And end peacefully my internal fight

Science in a Nutshell

What is the significance of breathing for life and body?

Breathing is the dance of the flow of air between life and death. Inhaling and exhaling are automatic activities that take place in our unconscious and are the basis of all our physical, mental, artistic and motional activity. The decisive proof that we stepped out of the mother's womb and stepped into life—and that we have departed from life—is breath, or the lack of it. According to Eastern philosophy, physical and mental health can only be maintained if Yin (the physical world), that is inhaling, and Yang (the world of energy where there is no physical substance), that is exhaling, are kept in balance. In Tao philosophy, this is called the equilibrium of wholeness, and advice is given to maintain it carefully. In Sanskrit, breath means *prana*, which also means life energy. In certain yoga exercises, the body's equilibrium is maintained by focusing on breathing. In the Shiva tradition of southern India, 24 different types of breathing and breath-regulating techniques are described. In Eastern culture breathing has been used to achieve body-awareness, healthy living and meditation for hundreds of years.

The approach to breathing in the Western world is mostly based on artistic (theatrical and musical) and scientific grounds. From an artistic perspective, breathing has been considered a communication method and a mode of transformation between different energy forms within the electromagnetic spectrum (1,2).

From a scientific point of view, breathing is one of the most vital bodily functions, which is being controlled involuntarily by the balance between oxygen and carbon dioxide in the brain stem and in the blood. When the depth and rate of breathing increases (hyperpnea) voluntarily or involuntarily (for instance during physical exercise), while the pressure of oxygen in the blood increases, there is no change in the pressure of carbon dioxide and the pH levels in the blood. However, in hyperventilation situations, where breathing is rapid and shallow—which occurs when we feel fear, stress and anxiety—the body does not get enough oxygen, leading to a distortion in the oxygen-carbon dioxide balance in the blood. Sympathetic stimulation causes shallow and rapid breathing: the bloodstream and the brain do not get enough oxygen. This causes shortness of breath, shivering and a choking feeling. The person gets into a vicious circle of rapid and shallow breathing, and the conditions get worse. According to published studies, hyperventilation syndrome, which can affect 10% of the population, can be easily rectified by slow and deep breathing, filling the diaphragm (3). Nevertheless, as will be explained below, studies show that voluntary hyperventilation can help with the treatment of some psychiatric illnesses, when conducted with the aid of an expert.

How does breathing happen? Mechanisms that drive breathing

Breathing is movement of air into (inspiration) and out (expiration) of the lungs, which occurs automatically and constantly under the brain stem's command. Breathing requires active participation of the diaphragm, chest and abdominal muscles. Ordinarily our breathing pace and type is adjusted automatically, depending on the levels of oxygen and carbon dioxide in the blood. Despite this, we can voluntarily adjust our breathing from the rapid and shallow breathing that occurs when we are excited due to stimulation by the sympathetic system to temporary deep and slow breathing, which enables us to calm down. The pranayamic breathing of voluntary slow and deep inhaling and holding the breath for a while (for about four seconds) and exhaling is the basis of all meditation methods used for combatting stress. With this method, it is possible to counteract the effect of the sympathetic system, which overstimulates the body and the nervous system, causing stress, by changing it to the calm condition activated by the parasympathetic system, which relaxes and blocks overstimulation (4-8). Also, it has been shown that by taking slow, deep breaths through the nose and holding the air for a while before exhaling (pranayamic breathing), theta and delta waves increase in the brain, as was explained in Chapter 1. Breathing resets, the adversely affected, over-stimulated activity, by positively affecting the heart, lungs and limbic system, as well as the cortex of the brain (8).

What is the function of breath control?

Breathing techniques that focus on deep and slow breathing, as part of complementary medicine, meditation and yoga, help to combat stress, increase oxygenation, lower blood pressure and heart rate, and calm the mind. For instance, statistically, breathing six times in 30 seconds can have a discernible effect on lowering the blood pressure and heart rate in patients suffering from high blood pressure (5,6).

In this way, we can engage the heart, lungs, limbic system and brain cortex so they work in harmony. It is also said that harmonious working of these organs helps with maintaining intracellular equilibrium (homeostasis), protecting the cells against over-stimulation (7,8). Studies have also shown that correct breathing methods can be instrumental in the treatment of psychiatric illnesses, anxiety, fear-induced post-traumatic stress disorder, insomnia, attention deficit disorder, depression and schizophrenia (9). Recovery is aided by the effects of deep breathing on the autonomic nervous system, emotion control, focus, awareness, and the decision-making mechanisms of the brain (9). This method has also proved effective in reducing the oxygen needs of the body (10). It has been shown that this method reduces the risk of cardiovascular illnesses, reduces the free radicals caused by oxidative stress, and is protective against many illnesses. It also increases neural plasticity (neural cell renewal) (11-14). It was also found that this method of breathing increased the IQ levels of children with developmental delays and aided in their social adaptation (13). It also positively affects the immune system.

Is our method of breathing important for our health?

The proportion of inhalation to exhalation matters. If we inhale and do not exhale sufficiently (as is the case in hyperventilation syndrome) we cannot discharge all the carbon dioxide in our blood and lungs. The carbon dioxide accumulated in our blood causes excessive stimulation of the nervous system and increased sympathetic activity. On the other hand, reduced carbon dioxide in the blood (hypocapnia), caused by rapid breathing, also referred to as hyperventilation, induces oxygen transfer to the brain, leading to dizziness and a tingling sensation.

We can moderate the autonomic system (sympathetic and parasympathetic system), which functions as a two-way bridge between the brain and the body, by regulating our breath, particularly by holding the breath for a while and exhaling slowly. Slowing down exhalation sends a signal to the heart to slow down and to the brain to reduce panic-inducing thoughts, reinstating our usual, relaxed condition and helping us maintain life balance. The breath held for a while (four seconds) and released slowly enables the enlargement of the alveoli, the little sacs where gas exchange occurs, facilitating the passage of oxygen into the bloodstream. This method of breathing is shown to decrease metabolism and oxygen consumption (15). Conversely, rapid and frequent breathing (hyperventilation) leads to an increase in sympathetic activity, causing stress in the body (16). Studies show that slow inhalation, holding the breath for a short time and prolonged exhaling, increases parasympathetic activity, which helps healing and cell renewal, as well as prompting slow brain waves (theta and delta) and the release of the melatonin hormone (16-18).

It is believed that the inhibiting signals that reduce excessive stimulation of the nervous system and connective tissue are responsible for the effects of pranayanic breathing at cellular level (8).

How important is the environment and the quality of air we breathe?

It is well known that the conditions in which we breathe are important for healthy living. Oxygen levels indoors are lower than outdoors in fresh air. Clean and fresh air is found in unpolluted environments where there are evergreen trees and at the seaside. It is known that after thunder, oxygen in the air is charged with negative ions. This is very beneficial; compared with recirculated air indoors, air charged with negative ions strengthens the cilia, the hair like protective brooms in the lungs, creates a feeling of well-being, prevents stress, enhances learning and positive feelings, creates resistance against germs by lowering body temperature as well as decreasing heart rate and breathing rate (19-23). In addition to this, breathing aromatic substances (phynocides) released into the air, particularly by trees, fruits and vegetables to protect the plants from bugs and germs, has significant benefits for strengthening the immune system and maintaining body equilibrium (24-26). Also, it is noteworthy that scientific studies have shown similar effects on the immune system of inhaling aromatic substances obtained from trees (such as citrus fragrance) (27).

Can voluntary hyperventilation be used in treatment?

With the Graf method, called holotopic breathing, developed in 1975, voluntary hyperventilation, focused body activity, and stimulating music can be used to bring to the conscious the emotionally damaging, suppressed memories held in the unconscious. This can raise the person's awareness and lead to emotional discharge, followed by relaxation and healing (28-30). This method suppresses the cortex, which is new in the evolutionary process, and activates the limbic system by rapid breathing, reduction in carbon dioxide and the ensuing change in blood pH, called alkalosis. This method does not have many adherents in the West, where there is a more rigid approach to medicine and studies are needed to prove its clinical efficacy.

In conclusion, it is suggested that the best method of breathing is uninterrupted, deep, calm, rhythmic breathing through the nose, by expanding the diaphragm muscles and holding the breath in for a while.

Many studies suggest that in cases of excessive stimulation of the sympathetic system and hyperventilation, deep breathing methods with a prolonged exhalation as well as a daily 15 to 20 minutes of regular voluntary diaphragmatic breathing have many beneficial effects on the body when stressed. These methods increase parasympathetic activity, which relaxes and nourishes the body and aids digestion. They should be systematically taught to patients and medical students, and practiced as a simple, easy, and free method of treatment.

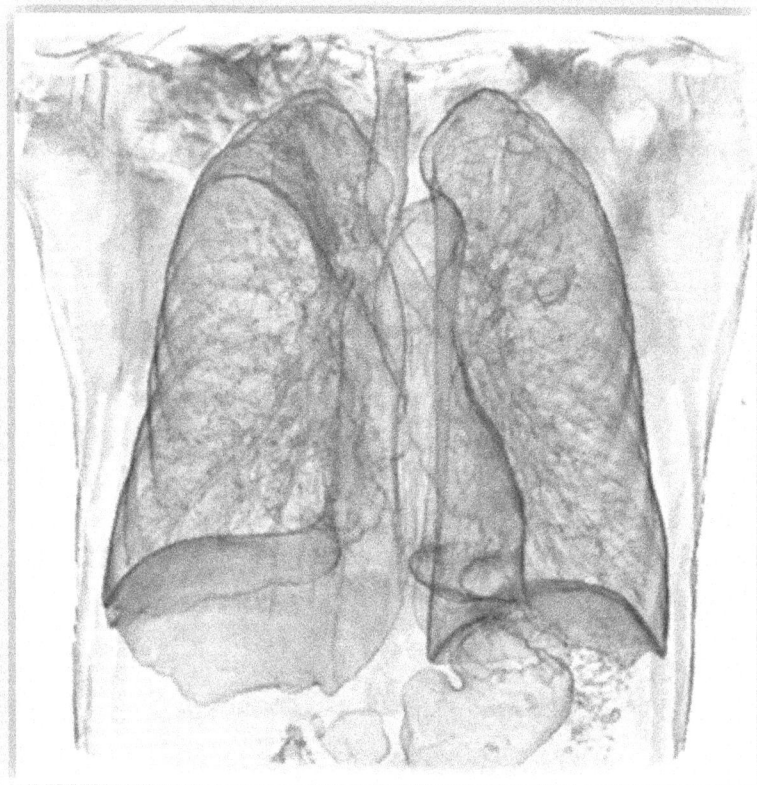

Picture 9.1: 3D lung images produced by a computed tomography scan, using X-rays, part of the electromagnetic spectrum

A Story and an Observation

Breathless

I'm on a plane journey between Ankara and Izmir. The atmosphere in the country is tense. People are quiet and contemplative. I am watching the clouds from the tiny window. All of a sudden there is an announcement asking whether there is a doctor for an ill passenger. I get up to see if I can help.

A young girl is lying on the floor in the aisle between the seats. Her eyes are closed. She does not react to the many urging voices. Other passengers are gathered around her, listing the medications they have that may help. I say, "There is no need for those." I sit on the floor and put the girl's head on my lap.

Her breathing is rapid, irregular and shallow. I hold her hands and whisper in her ear:

"Don't worry! You are safe. We are looking after you. Now focus only on your breathing; take slow, deep breaths. Just follow your breathing. Prolong your exhalation."

The ill girl follows my instructions. We synchronize our breathing for a few minutes. After a while she comes to and begins to cry. I ask her name. She doesn't reply but apologizes while squeezing my hand. She sits up. There is a tattoo on her neck which reads "Ataturk."

I whisper in her ear, "You are strong, everything is under control. You are a daughter of Ataturk."

I tell the girl she can now take back control...

The girl opens her eyes, apologizes once more.

I reassure the girl, "These things can happen, it's normal," and leave the girl at her seat, to allow her time to recover.

Merely breathing solves the problem without medication and further fuss.

Once more, I think of how breathing can heal with its miraculous power, how it can calm down the panic created by our turbulent thoughts. We glide slowly over the clouds in the sky…

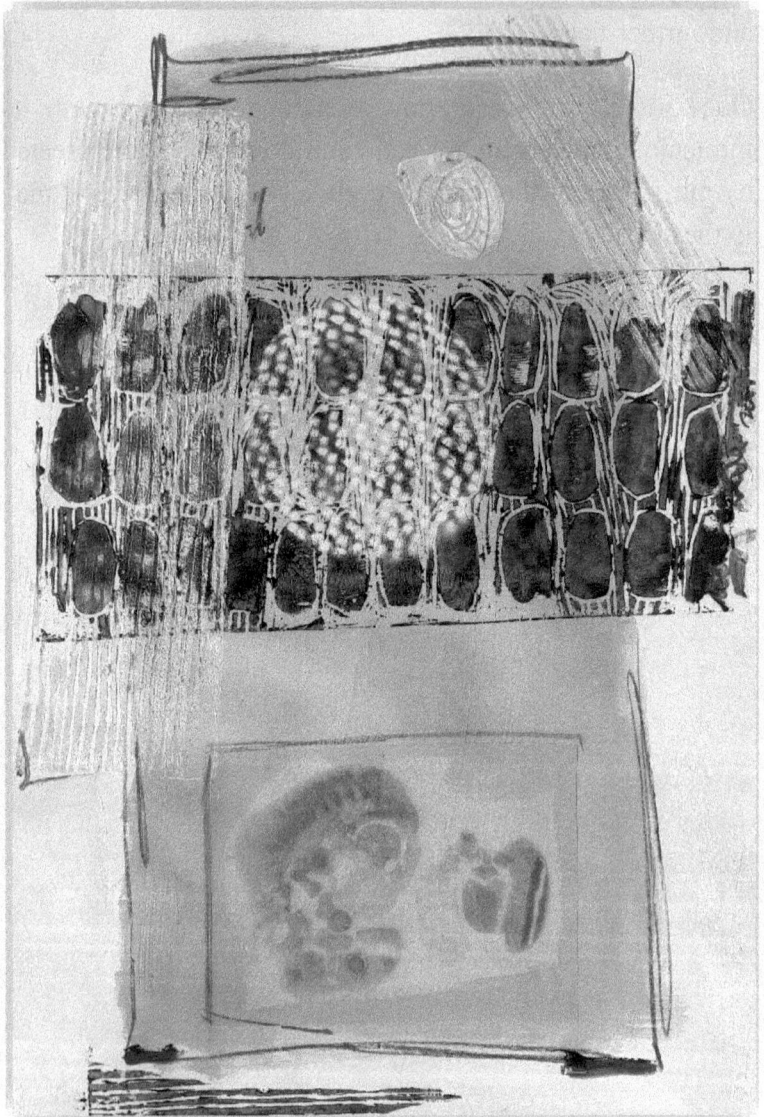

Art Picture 9: M. Soylemez, 'Breathing of cell'

When you have only two pennies left in the world, buy a loaf of bread with one and a lily with the other.
Chinese proverb

10 - PERCEPTION, LIGHT AND AESTHETICS

Senses

Feel how your eyes' windows
Open to the universe, ever curious;
How your sight illuminates the darkness;
How scent of rose passes through your nostrils
And is directed into hidden channels

Sense how the touch of warm water
Soothes your cheek;
How the soft breeze, a flutter
Caresses your skin.

Let your tongue move in resonance
With the melodic romance
Of a tune that will entrance:
All living things join in love's dance.

Science in a Nutshell

How does our brain sense the electromagnetic spectrum?

Our sensory organs, the intermediaries that enable us to communicate with the world, are the windows of our brain, opening to the universe, and the receptors of the portion of the electromagnetic spectrum we can sense. Like a wireless device, they receive and transmit information.

Our sensory organs, with the aid of their receptors, are instrumental in various interactions, emotions and thoughts in our brain and body. The senses and the brain are parts of a whole. The data only becomes meaningful after being processed in the brain. If the brain hasn't developed the ability to process any given data, or if the relevant part is damaged, even if the sensory organ is not damaged the data cannot be computed into meaningful information. The proportion of space reserved in the brain for these sensory receptions is illustrated in picture 10.1. In terms of the space allocated in our brain the hands, tongue and lips get the biggest share. The feet are allocated much less space in the brain (Picture 10.1).

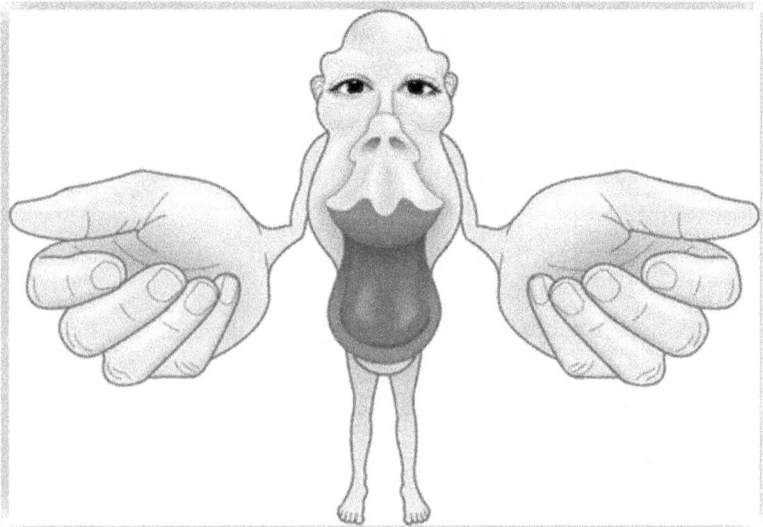

Picture 10.1: Homunculus. A representation of the human body based on the proportion of brain space dedicated to sensory functions for various parts of the body. The body parts that are used the most for sensing (hands, thumb, lips and tongue) are represented proportionately bigger and the less used parts (such as torso and back) are smaller.

Do the senses always tell the truth?

Senses, primarily the eyes, can easily be affected by disturbances of perception; what we see or hear is subjective. Until the 1800s it was assumed that our senses always recorded the truth, but then German physiologist Johannes Müller proved that human senses and perceptions can be distorted. We should be aware that our senses can be misleading, which will allow us to take a more flexible attitude towards ourselves and the others (1).

How does the electromagnetic spectrum's visible light affect us?

Visible light, an element of the electromagnetic spectrum, primarily affects the eye; it carries energy in waves or photons, but it has no mass. Light is one-trillionth of the electromagnetic spectrum, yet it is one of the waves which gives us the most information about our world. The light of the visible spectrum is sensed and processed in our brain, in either its simplest form or in the colors of the rainbow—violet having the highest energy, at one end, and red the lowest energy.

The eyes contain specialized cells that can sense the light (Picture 10.2). These are called rods and cones, which convert light into images, and melanopsin cells, which convert light into information regarding time of day, so as to adjust the body's circadian rhythm. When our eyes convert light into images, it works just like a camera. The light that enters the eye is first refracted by the lens and reflected onto a screen called the retina. On this screen there are millions of photoreceptor cells, just like the receptor in a digital camera. When the light from these receptor cells hits the rods and cones, the molecular configurations of the cells change, and they start producing electric signals. The electrical signals are subsequently transmitted as image data by the nerve cells and then the nerves to the relevant parts of the brain, enabling the formation of the vision (2,3)

Picture 10.2: The nerve cells, which carry the information to the vision nerves. The rods (white) and cone (green-pink) cells in the retina. When light enters through the eyes it's reflected on a screen called the retina, then detected and transmitted to the nerve cells by the rod and cone cells.

Melanopsin-expressing retinal ganglion cells, which are the third type of cells that detect the light, play a significant role in adjusting our life rhythm according to the light level. Signals from these cells stimulate the pineal gland, which is also known as *the third eye*. The melatonin hormone released from this gland affects our body's health in a positive way (4-7).

In addition to our circadian rhythm, functions such as how our pupils react to light, our emotions, sleep, perceptions and differentiating light occur as a result of the melanopsin cells' activity. It has been shown through various studies that these cells are damaged in glaucoma and Alzheimer's patients (4).

Depending on the position of the objects around us, the cells in the retina can adjust the refraction of light by the lens, with signals sent to the brain, in a fashion similar to that of binoculars. The pupils dilate and contract, depending on the amount of ambient light, to stabilize the amount of light entering the eyes. The cells in the retina can also adjust their own sensitivity depending on the amount of light present. Our range and sense of vision change in a dynamic way, depending on our brain function and attention.

How does light interact with our third eye and brain?

The melanopsin cells that sense the light are directly related to the pineal gland and contain cells similar to those in the eye. The melatonin hormone is released by this gland at night, when there is no light. Its levels are low during the day. It has been proven that this hormone protects against cancer and many other illnesses, stimulates growth, and adjusts the sleep rhythm as well as our metabolism. In blind people, due to lack of light stimulation, melatonin is released in higher proportions. According to studies, cancer is less prevalent in blind people compared with society as a whole (8). Melanopsin is most sensitive to blue-violet light with the shortest wavelength and highest frequency (4). For this reason, it is suggested that working in an environment where there is blue or artificial light, as well as working at night and sleeping during the day, reduce the release of melatonin (9). In addition to the third eye (pineal gland), light is directly connected to the suprachiasmatic nucleus and hypothalamus, the regions of the brain that affect our emotions.

What relationship is there between light and illness?

Melatonin is a hormone that prevents cancer and tumors from forming and growing. It's worth noting that it's important to keep a balance between melatonin and estrogen. It is well established that the frequency of breast cancer in women who work at night is higher (8-11). As well as the cancer-preventing effect of melatonin, it is also suggested that it has an important role in preventing cardiovascular diseases, tinnitus, migraine, diabetes and premature aging. It has an effect on the neuron cells in the brain, which can be effective in preventing Parkinson's, Alzheimer's and ischemia. It also reduces the risk of infections and diabetes and stimulates the immune system in a positive way (8-13).

Are there any melatonin sources other than the pineal gland?

Melatonin is also released from the retina, though to a lesser degree than from the pineal gland. Additionally, many foods are good sources of melatonin. The most important of these foods are milk consumed at nighttime, eggs, fish, grape skin, mushrooms, coffee, cacao, peanuts and hazelnuts. The artificial melatonin taken as a supplement in pill form is reported to be less effective (14).

How do eyes operate as the windows of the brain?

Eyes, which from the inside are like windows opening into the universe, can also be peered into from the outside, conveying information about the body and the brain

(Picture 2). The veins in our eyes, and the retina where light is reflected are like a cinema screen, giving clues as to what is happening in our bodies. Physicians can observe what is happening by dilating the pupils. It is possible to diagnose vascular diseases and diabetes by analyzing the veins in the eyes and the retina.

How does light interact with our bodies other than with our eyes? Can cells generate light?

There's increasing evidence that light, described as photons, affects the whole body, and that cells generate photons called biophotons. In addition, it is suggested that cells use photons to communicate. Communication by photons has also been identified in bacteria, plants, and kidney cells (15). Similar properties have been observed in nerve cells. In experiments carried out on mice it was observed that spinal cord cells transmitted light. It is well established that in many cells, particularly in the mitochondria responsible for energy metabolism, there are many photosensitive cells called chromophores. It is also suggested that light interacts with the cellular fluid and the cell membrane. In particular, it is claimed that the filament-like microtubules that form the skeleton of nerve and muscle cells carry and transmit light in the same manner as fiber-optic cables. There is growing evidence that, in addition to the usual method of electrical and biochemical transmission by the nerve cells, they also use photons to generate signals. The discipline of science called *biophotonics* is making rapid progress in understanding the interaction of photons with biological structures.

How do light and aesthetics interact with our sensory brain?

While light and color in our environment cause the above effects in our brain and body, they also activate an internal perception called aesthetics. The discipline that examines the interaction of this perception with the brain is called *neuroesthetics*. We compare and interpret the external environment with the feelings of our internal aesthetic perception and try to put the external environment in order. This perception is activated by our awareness of our internal aesthetics. We reflect our perception of aesthetics and beauty, which we harmonize with nature, to our environment, and blend it with materials to turn it into art (16).

What does the science of brain and beauty perception, neuroesthetics, teach us?

Can we take a photo of our thoughts and senses?

Every type of physical stimulation, particularly light, that is created by the electromagnetic spectrum is processed in our brain, turning it into a sense that affects our life and body. The scientific discipline that examines, using scientific methods, how this sense is formed and how it interacts with our body and physiology is called neuroesthetics. For instance, when you show a pretty face to humans, the parts of the brain that are stimulated by this can be shown through brain mapping, or functional magnetic resonance imaging (fMRI) (Picture 10. 3). In other words, we really can take a picture of our senses and thoughts (17). It has been proved that pretty pictures stimulate the reward center in the brain (e.g. nucleus accumbens) and increase motivation. It's also been shown that we are born with a universal sense of beauty, which is intrinsic to humans irrespective of culture and race (18-20).

In summary, the visual system, responsible for processing light on the electromagnetic spectrum, forms a sensory organ that affects our life, body, emotions and life cycle, in harmony with our circadian clock. Other than the two eyes that extend from the outer world to our brain, the pineal gland, which is referred to as the third eye and has similar cellular properties to the eye, by releasing melatonin, protects us from illnesses such as cancer, as well as regenerating and rejuvenating us.

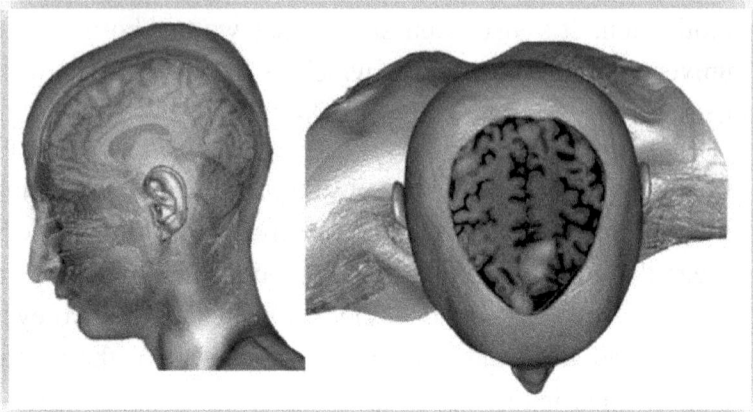

Picture 10.3: Samples of images of Brain Mapping or Functional Magnetic Resonance Imaging which use the radio waves of the electromagnetic spectrum.

The red areas show the regions in the brain stimulated by thoughts and senses. This essentially provides a photo of the brain's thoughts and senses.

A Story and an Observation

Visual Chat With The Quince Tree

While my body was watching a quince tree
it said,
'Life is so deep,
earth so rich;
feelings so ripe;
I cannot get enough of life
like you, quince tree,
to understand existence.
I watch while a qanun plays
the rivulets of water on your trunk
the joy of birds dancing in your branches
the ants
hurrying on your bark…'

Cannot get enough of life's taste,
the light reflecting my face
like a mirror
of the shimmering leaves.
Why did you decide to display your beauty?
First you strung fresh green almond leaves in an array on
the elegant branches
like the necks of swans
And afterwards the light pink blossoms popped open like
the birth of a baby.
Why are you so beautiful?
Was there a point to being so pretty?
After all, it's only for the bees and butterflies.
What are you trying to tell them with your blooms?
Or are you trying to satisfy the human soul first?
Will you spread visions in front of their eyes?
Each bloom will turn into a baby quince
getting tastier by the day.
Then a cheeky boy will
bite into your crunchy, juicy flesh.

Your children will blend into the human children,
As all living beings blend into each other.
This cycle will continue until humans turn all fruit groves
into concrete blocks.
And you will watch quietly
as it unfurls around you...

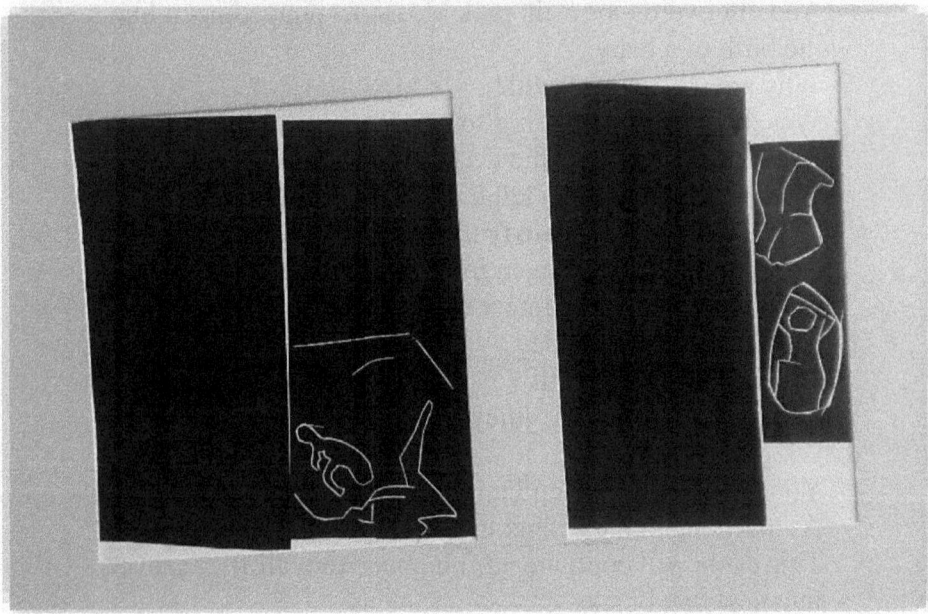

Art Picture 10: M. Soylemez 'Darkness'

Odors have such powers of persuasion that they are more powerful than words, seeing with own eyes, emotions and willpower.

Patrick Süskind

11 - ODOR, BRAIN AND BODY

Baby, muslin and scent

A true story that grabbed the ears
About a crying baby and mother with angel wings
The mother lost her way during a chaotic birth
One body did not live, the other remained on earth

The baby is left alone to persevere;
No breast milk, no smell of mother, he sobs in fear
The midwives are helpless, finding no way to cheer
The child drawn away from earth's sphere

The baby bottles, the wet nurses are to no avail
He needs his mother in order to prevail,
When all the efforts of others to end his wail fail
They surrender to a wise woman's call for a veil.

The midwife asks for the muslin the mother wore on her
head
Spreads it over the baby's face, as a curtain net, between
life and death.
The baby finds peace with his mother's scent
That calms his soul, which wants to escape

Meanwhile a breeze whispers, even to ears that are deaf
Carries the muslin's magic scent, through the baby's calm
breath
Takes the baby's soul, binds him to the whole after death
And lets flutter only two leaves of a tree in dreamland.

Science in a Nutshell

What is odor, and how does it affect the body?

Smelling involves sensing, by the nose, chemical molecules vibrating in the air. It is believed that when we notice a smell we are really sensing vibrations of the molecules, in other words waves. The organ for smelling is a member of the limbic system, which, in evolutionary development, belongs to the oldest part of the brain, along with anger, hatred, nausea, fear, appetite, sexuality, memory. It is one of the most powerful and principal sensory organs, which both humans and animals use directly for survival. This sense affects our life physically, emotionally, psychologically as well as socially. Odor is transmitted to the frontal lobe of the brain by many short olfactory nerves (Picture 11.1) These nerves are connected to the limbic system and are probably the only nerves belonging to the unconscious brain. We distinguish hundreds of odors from one another and make connections between those odors and our memories. Our emotional state is greatly affected by odors. While pleasant odors may cheer us up, foul odors cause revulsion and negative emotions (1).

What are the properties of our own odor?

Each of us has a signature odor, like a unique fingerprint, made up of hundreds of chemicals. A person's odor changes according to hormones, physical activity, the environment, what the person has eaten. It even reflects emotions and excitement.

How does odor affect our life?

Odor is one of the principal factors affecting our social relationships and the degree of rapport we establish with other humans. Newborns can distinguish their mother's odor from the others shortly after they are born. Moreover, it was observed that these babies choose cloths rubbed in mother's milk over clean ones (2). Odor also plays an important role in choosing a partner. Studies have established that the type of tissue (major histocompatibility complex, MHC) has a role in the odor released by the genes. Living beings that can choose partners in natural environments generally choose, by distinguishing between sweat odors, partners with different tissues than their own, thus showing a preference for genetic variation and hybrid vigor (2,3). Odor generally gives clues about age, gender, fertility, identity, emotions and health by influencing our unconscious. Studies have found that a person can identify clothes that have been worn by their partner from those of others, by distinguishing their odor.

Can odor help with the diagnosis of illnesses?

Just like animals, humans can distinguish bad from good, harmful from harmless by using the olfactory sense. It is estimated that humans have the ability to distinguish between approximately 10,000 odors. This ability is more developed in cats and dogs. The use of dogs as an effective method for diagnosing cancers started with diagnosing breast cancer. Studies showed that specially trained dogs can identify the urine of prostate or liver cancer patients with up to 100% accuracy (4-6).

How is aroma used in our physical health and treatment of illnesses?

The origins of therapy employing aromatic plant oils and other aromatic compounds, dubbed aromatherapy, can be traced back as far as Ancient Egypt. The Arabs, Chinese, Germans and the French made use of scents for treatment. Current scientific studies have shown that aroma therapies using materials such as nigella seed oil (nigella sativa), lavender (lavandula anguvstifolia), eucalyptus(eucalyptus globulus), mint (menthe piperita), rosemary (rosmarinus officinalis), arabic jasmine(jasminium sambac), and black pepper (piper nigrum) may have significant effects in the treatment of psychiatric illnesses and illnesses affecting the brain, such as dementia and Alzheimer's (8-14). Aromatherapy is also used to deal with stress, labor pains, high blood pressure, post-operation nausea and vomiting (15-20).

In Alzheimer's patients, who are increasing in number throughout the world, it has been shown that the olfactory sense is significantly diminished. It is observed that aromatherapy calms down such patients and reduces the use of tranquilizers. In experiments carried out using lavender and rosemary, it was established that aromatherapy increased memory ability, slowed the progress of Alzheimer's disease and possibly protects from developing dementia (22). In animal tests of the thyme essential oil used in aromatherapy, it was found that it could prevent harmful plaque formation in veins (anti-amyloid) and breakdown of the chemicals needed for neural signal transmission (anticholin esterases) and reduce inflammation (anti-inflammatory) from the effects of stress (antioxidant)

124

(23). It is thought that it is effective in Alzheimer's disease because of these properties.

In studies on dementia, patients were shown to have benefited from primarily lavender, as well as melissa, lemon, tangerine, rosemary, orange, mint and geranium essences. It was revealed that aromas such as lavender, tree, or forest scents reduce activity in the prefrontal cortex of the brain, leading to a reduction in stress levels. Likewise, many studies have shown that the lavender scent has a preventative effect on inflammation, headache, stress and depression (21).

It is also established that some aromatic compounds that exist in the air (phytoncides) and aromatic substances similar to these, such as pinene and limonene, obtained from evergreen trees, as well as cryptomeria japonica and cedar, taken in through the olfactory system, strengthen the immune system (24).

In summary, the olfactory system, which acts like an extension of our brain, is the most principal and oldest sense we possess. This is the only sensory organ that is directly linked to the limbic system, the most primitive and fundamental system in our brain. Although it is difficult to measure and distinguish by scientific methods, its impact on our physical and mental health, as well as our life in general, is immense. Olfactory-based treatments deserve more emphasis and should be developed as a pleasant and beneficial method. Aromatherapy has no side effects other than possible allergies. It is a simple, cheap, easily accessible treatment method, employing the richness and beauty of nature, which adds happiness and depth to life.

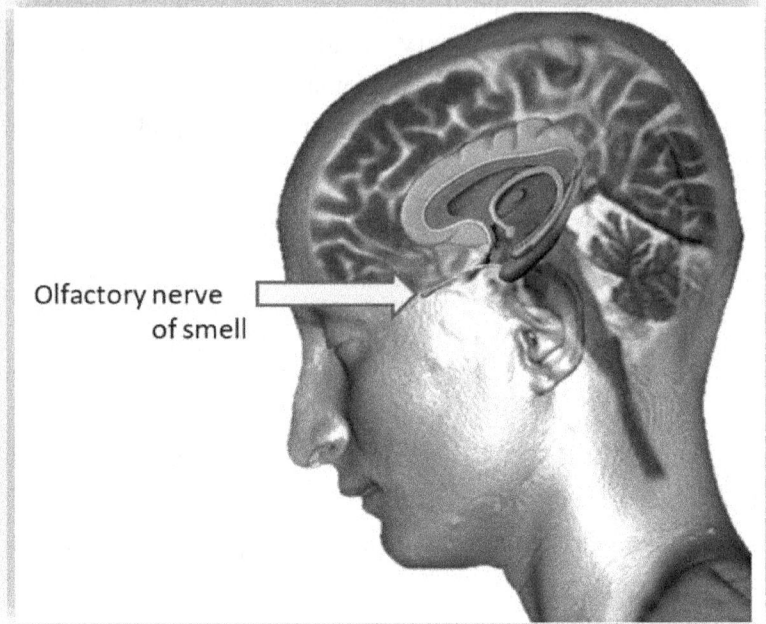

Picture 11.1: The olfactory nerve, which is part of the limbic system, is related to emotions and memory, and is directly linked to the brain.

A Story and an Observation

Lavender-Scented Auntie Zuleyha

Three daughters, three sons-in-law, seven grandchildren, one cat, a lemon tree in the garden that bears fruit without ever getting tired...

These are all tucked away in a high-walled, whitewashed, low-ceilinged stone house with a range in the kitchen. They are all hidden in this house along with a hard-working, marble-skinned woman called Zuleyha, whose youthful beauty was much remarked upon years ago.

Ever since the daughter-in-law arrived, some years have seemed to pass quickly, others less so. This house, with its row of plates lined up on a shelf, long divans with hand-made lace covers, the stove, the black and white photo of the man of the house hung on its whitewashed walls, this house which has embraced much laughter and tears, hens and even cows in the past, tells the story of Auntie Zuleyha.

The daughters of Auntie Zuleyha are grief-stricken: "Our mum confuses our names. We wash her feet, she tells us off for not washing the other one. She insists on giving a bracelet to our already married sister when she marries. When she goes out, she cannot find her way back. She constantly talks to our father in the photo, who died five years ago. This upsets us a lot. None of the medication worked. Do you think there is a cure?"

I look at Auntie Zuleyha; she is cheerful, not caring a bit about anything going on around her. She is wearing gold earrings and bangles—a well-adorned, 85-year-old blushing bride. She keeps on telling her daughters she wants to leave. I give the lavender eau de cologne which I brought with me to Auntie Zuleyha. She carefully opens her wrinkled and trembling palms. The cologne is sprinkled in her palms, and the scent fills the room. All other palms are opened, ready for me. They all inhale the cologne. Auntie Zuleyha's eyes close for a while and open slowly.

Auntie Zuleyha, who has paid no attention to me since my arrival, stares at me. She leaves her imaginary husband and starts to engage with me. "Who are you? Where did you come from? Let's go out for a walk," she says, inching forward to me with a cheeky smile. She will run in the fields and play tip-cat, playhouse and sidewalk chalk games.

I hold her hand, I feel the palpation of her vein that has been working incessantly for many years; I feel the excitement buried inside her. "So, I hear you cannot sleep at night?" I ask. She shakes her head, "While everyone sleeps at night I cannot sleep a wink. Your uncle wanders around me." Afterwards, it seems she slowly starts to gather her wits.

The chatting goes on and on; coffee is drunk, fortunes are told, Turkish delights are served while the daughters and grandchildren run around in pleasant excitement. Auntie Zuleyha's daughters talk about the vineyards with lavender plants of her youth. When there was an abundance of grape molasses, dried grapes and layers of dried fruit pulp, Auntie Zuleyha never suffered from insomnia.

While the words flutter in the air like butterflies, I watch Auntie Zuleyha's trembling hands and attentive eyes. "Next week, I have a surprise for you," I say before I leave.

I buy a piece of yellow chambray fabric with lavender patterns and a lot of dried lavender from the spice store and prepare a pillow big enough for two people to rest their heads on. With the lavender pillow tucked in my bag, making a slight swishing sound, I follow the route to the stone house, hoping to catch the memory cleared by the scent of lavender.

As before, big smiles and tight hugs welcome me into the house. I take out the surprise present from my bag. "Look, Auntie Zuleyha, this is a pillow I made for you. Smell it. It smells of the scent you love. Do you remember? Like the lavender-scented vineyard of your youth. From now on you will put your head on this pillow and fall asleep like a baby. When you cannot sleep it will bring back memories of your lavender-scented vineyard." The daughters take the pillow joyfully and place it in a prominent corner. Auntie Zuleyha sizes me and the pillow up for a long time. I leave, saying, "We'll find out if it works."

I start calling the daughters every day. "How was it? Did she sleep last night?"

"Yes, yes, there were no complaints or movement from her room. We checked her every now and then, and she was sleeping comfortably. Also, now it seems she remembers us a bit better, because she talks about sensible things like she used to. She sits her grandchildren on her lap, and this makes us happy. We don't understand what has happened. Is it the result of that pillow?"

"Yes," I reply, "I think it was the lavender-scented pillow that connected Auntie Zuleyha back to life. Her head found rest on that pillow."

From this end of the telephone I visualize Auntie Zuleyha among the lavender scents. I feel her wandering in the vineyards and gardens as if she is in a deep sleep. Who knows, maybe in a pleasant and happy dreamland…

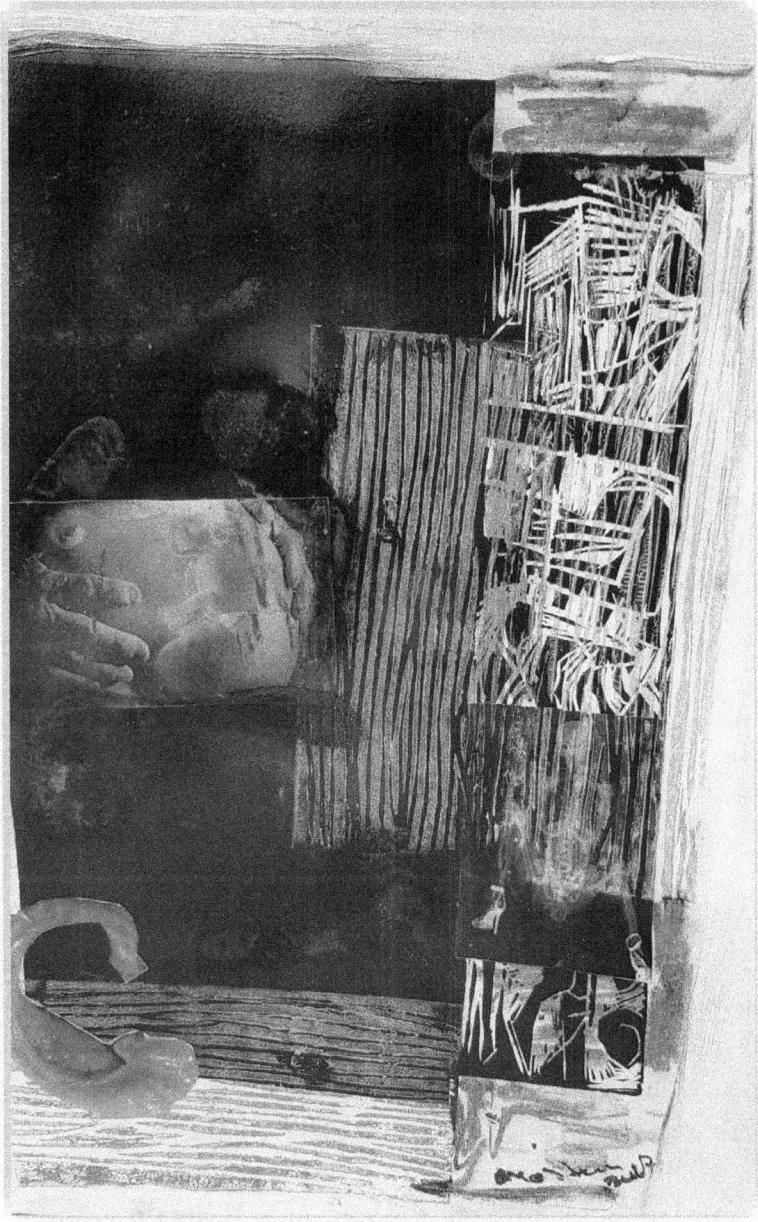

Art Picture 11: M. Soylemez "Hands, Touch and memory"

Only the person who knows the delicacy of touching
can reflect the delicacy of their own soul and body.
George Eliot

12 - TOUCHING AND HEALING

Plea to the healer

Touch me,
First with your eyes
Then with your voice
Then with your hands

Let touch flow
From the body to your hands
To your intuition
And subconscious mind

Feel how touch can heal
An internal peal
Provoking to feel
The spirit and body in real

Science in a Nutshell

What is touch, and what purpose does it serve?

Touch is a cognitive, emotional and social sense. The skin that covers our entire body is an intermediary as well as the biggest receptor and transmitter of this sense. The sense of touch that our skin holds is the most basic source of the relationship we form with other living beings, our environment and ourselves. It includes pain. While this sense is useful in distinguishing and identifying objects, localizing and moving them, facilitating our lives, it also serves as the most important means of pleasure and communication. For this reason, it is a fundamental determinant in our social relationships. In other words, our touch organ is a social organ. Researchers found that a monkey who wasn't able to touch his mother showed symptoms of stress and didn't develop properly. Touch is one of the most fundamental elements of the relationship between the child and parents. It is the source of happiness and pleasure. Holding the hand of a loved one reduces stress and anxiety and is relaxing (1).

Why is touching pleasant and healing?

While touching causes relaxation in the body, it also contributes to healing and growth. It has been proven in both humans and animals that happiness and reward hormones such as oxytocin, endorphins, and dopamine play a role in this pleasure. Studies reveal that particularly attentive and tender touching causes a sensation of pleasure in humans and that this sensation is transmitted to the brain by C tactile (CT) receptor neurons, which are unmyelinated (2,3). CT neurons are predominantly present in the hairy skin and more concentrated on the face, arms and legs. Studies using functional MRI techniques found that the sensory signals transmitted by such neutrons stimulate the orbitofrontal cortex and posterior insula parts of the brain (4-6). The insula links the limbic system and parietal lobe, forming a sense of reward and protecting homeostasis in the body (7-8).

How does the touch sense function as a social communication method?

As mentioned above, our skin also acts as a medium of social communication, relaying our emotions. As well as feelings of pleasure, it can also mediate stress and discontent. When our finger burns, we touch the hurting part with our tongue or the other hand to reduce the pain. We apply the same method to other living beings we think are suffering. Interactions such as a handshake and touch usually aid in trust and good social relations between people, as well as inspiring feelings of cooperation (3). We use this sense to show our love and give attention to our own body and to our loved ones. Touch, which also affects the unconscious, is one of the most primitive and principal universal communication methods between humans as well as between humans and animals or plants.

How is touch relayed to the brain?

There are nerve receptors in our skin, like the CT neurons but located deeper, that sense vibrations and pressure such as massage (Vater Pacini and Meissner corpuscles). These receptors consist of ball-like skeins formed of layers of nerve cells (Picture 12.1). They relay the sense of touch directly to the nerves and then to the brain. Touching the skin means, in effect, touching the nerve endings and sending signals indirectly to the brain. The sense of touch can be measured in scientific studies by the microneurography method and standardized to carry out many experiments (3-7).

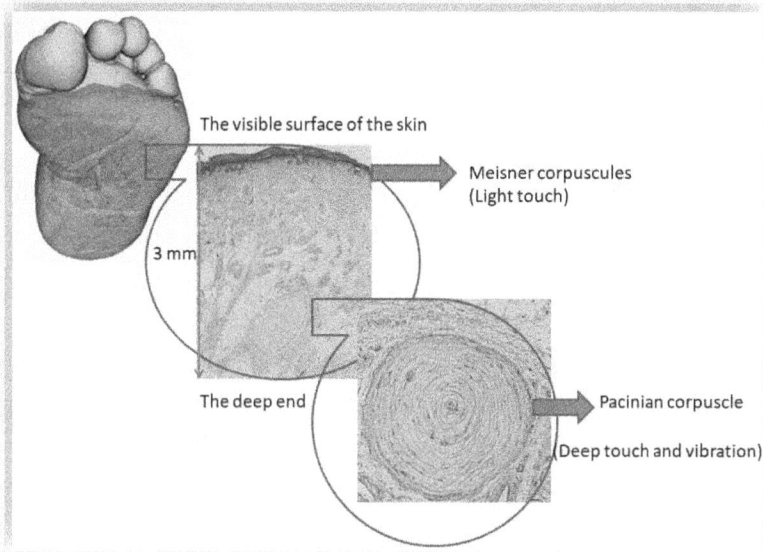

Picture 12.1. The image, under a light microscope, of a normal skin sample taken from the sole of the foot. Beneath the surface of the skin are the small skeins of Meisner corpuscles, which are responsible for sensing mild touch; a few millimeters underneath are the onion or skein-like deep Pacini corpuscles, nestling in the fat layer, which respond to deep pressure and vibration.

Is touch used in medicine and curing diseases?

Identifying and curing illnesses by touching has been a known method in medicine for centuries and is used to calm the patient. A hands-on examination of the patient by the physician is one of the most basic methods of medicine. In recent years, because medicine is becoming more mechanical and because patient numbers have risen, examination by hand and touch has become less frequent. Despite this, complementary medicine continues to use touch and massage therapy to heal and relax patients.

It has been shown that touch or massage therapy is effective over a wide spectrum of ages and illnesses; that is, from a premature infant to an elderly person suffering from dementia (9).

It has been proven to have positive clinical effects in premature infants and babies who have undergone a minor procedure. It has been shown that massage therapy facilitated growth, reduced symptoms of stress, strengthened the immune system and increased the pain threshold in babies by activating the parasympathetic system (increasing the vagal tone), and enabled such patients to be discharged quicker from the hospital (10-12).

In the same manner, it has been shown that massage is the most effective emotional stimulant in children with behavior disorders and autism. Massage therapies are used to reduce stress levels, relax the patient, inspire trust and feelings of well-being, relax the muscles, encourage the growth and development of children, reduce pain, lethargy, nausea, anxiety, or the feeling of stress, and to correct sleep disorders and ease side effects of pregnancy (13-15). In studies carried out on late-stage cancer patients with bone metastases, an entire body massage reduced feelings of pain and anxiety with no side effects within 15 to 20 minutes (13-15). In other studies, supporting these findings, it was revealed that the feeling of relaxation can last from a few hours up to 24 hours after the massage (16-17).

How does touching other living beings affect humans?

It is scientifically proven that when a person touches and interacts with animals for a while, it increases happiness hormones and reduces stress hormones (18). In another scientific study it was shown that touching the leaves of vegetables, fruits or other plants caused feelings of relaxation and calm in the unconscious of humans (19-20).

Consequently, touching humans and plants can reduce or cure the symptoms of illnesses such as pain by relaxing and arousing feelings of healing, trust and happiness in the body. In this day and age, when the time a physician can devote to a patient is reduced, and frequently machines are used to examine patients, knowing the benefits of and using this basic sense will increase both patient and physician satisfaction, enhance medical treatments, establish rapport and trust between the patient and the physician, and facilitate placebo healing.

A Story and an Observation

The light that touched Tarik

A shanty house in Mamak.

A house with a crooked chimney spewing gnarled smoke, whitewashed, with wonky bricks, geraniums in the windows, and the warmth of people in the rooms...

In this small, warm house, two people are hugging each other: a man and a woman. Still devoted after many years together, their hearts beat with one wish while they talk to the geraniums in the window: "A baby with tiny hands."

Years go by and the wish still lives in their hearts; as their bodies see half a century go by, the wish spills out into the universe.

The storks who brought the baby dropped Tarik into his mother's lap on a cold winter day: a beautiful-faced, beautiful-eyed, white marble-skinned baby, as sweet as cotton candy.

The mother, in her mature age, who hadn't seen a baby's face before, started suckling the baby. The child grew and grew but kept his distance from the neighbors' children. The neighbors sized him up and down, and kept their children away from this boy, whose hands and arms were moving in a weird fashion.

As Tarik grew older, the sounds coming out of his mouth wouldn't turn into words. He would never make eye contact, nor be able to use his arms and legs properly. The sad mother and tired father went from one doctor to another, looking for a cure for their son, asking, "Why doesn't our son talk, why doesn't he feed himself, why does he pull the girls' hair and kick the boys and never make eye contact with us?"

The wise doctors examined Tarik. They said when he came out of his mother's womb, his brain was starved of oxygen. Feeling helpless, they held Tarik's little hands and made their way home.

Tarik could express himself in his own way using his arms and legs. Then he turned 7, and the authorities knocked on their door one day to say it was time to go to school.

They sent Tarik to a school which had an ancient sycamore tree in its garden. Tarik touched that tree every day as he was passing by. Perhaps because of that tree, he didn't scream or cry to resist going to school. They put Tarik in a classroom among children who were different from everybody else, who were damaged yet cheerful, who could not speak nor hear, who could not walk nor eat by themselves. Tarik was surprised by this. He was scared of the crowd, of not having his mother nor father, of not seeing the geraniums. He pulled the girls' hair, kicked the boys, broke all the crockery on the table. The educators put Tarik in a corner, built a wall around him with desks, like a prison. In their haste to finish other tasks, they forgot the little boy there.

While the other children were taken to the garden or to the market, Tarik was left in his corner. Withdrawing from life around him, he expressed his anger with his kicks and frothing at the mouth.

One day a school inspector turned up unannounced. He did not like the circumstances of the classroom. He pointed at Tarik and asked the head teacher, "Haven't you got any teachers who can get through to this child?" The head teacher thought for a long time about what could be done, how they could touch Tarik's life, then thought of the kind-hearted teacher Sevil.

Sevil, as her name implied, was loved by everyone, and was asked to take charge of this boy that no one wanted to touch. With a kind heart and a desire "to touch the life of this child," she stroked Tarik's head every day. She held his hand, touched her nose to his nose. Every time he threw a kick, she cuddled the child without worrying about his saliva and snot.

At every touch of their noses, Tarik started to form a bond with his teacher like the one he had with his mother, the sycamore tree, the geraniums. He started to have eye contact with others. Observers were taken aback by this change in him.

As days passed, the bond with Seville turned into a desire to survive, to learn, to live and understand. In time, Tarik learned not to kick, not to pull girls' hair, to control his body, and to make eye contact with others.

His expressionless face started to smile; he used his legs to walk; his hands, with which he used to pull hair, he now used to hold a pencil. His imprisonment turned into an adventure when he started to go to the market. Tarik started to observe and understand the simple beauty of daily life. While Tarik was watching the world around him, others started to understand and love Tarik. The mirror that teacher Sevil held to Tarik illuminated the hidden side of this seemingly helpless boy and brought out its beauty.

Sevil's hand, touching Tarik's head, her nose touching his nose, were in fact touching a pure soul finally embracing the world around it.

Art Picture 12. M. Soylemez "The Shadow of Death

If you inject music and love in people's lives
you can heal them.
Bob Marley

13 - TOUCHING WITH SOUND: MUSIC (HEALING WITH MUSIC)

Healing with Music

That melodic happiness
Touches our hearts, resonating wholeness
And vibrates in us endless
Cures the body ceaseless

When doors are opened to the rhythm of resonance,
The body's molecules dance with brilliance,
Healing power awakening in each cell
A mysterious internal journey begins
Towards a harmonizing mystical spell.

Science in a Nutshell

Can music be used for our health?

When applied in accordance with its purpose and by people trained in the subject, music can play a role in curing illness. This has been proven in clinical and scientific studies that have entered the treatment guidebooks (1,2).

Next to the radio frequency on the electromagnetic spectrum, music is an interesting stimulant that has been used as a treatment method for many centuries and interacts with the whole body. The human ear can hear sound waves on the low energy region of the electromagnetic spectrum with a frequency between 20 and 20 thousand vibrations per second. Music is within this range.

It has been shown that certain types of music have a calming effect, guarding against stress and epilepsy (3). However, it has also been shown that some types of music trigger epilepsy. For such reasons, music is an alternative medicine method that needs to be used with a full awareness of its effects.

What are the properties of healing music?

Studies carried out with music revealed that patients benefited from light and flowing melodies, with a beat ranging between 60 and 80 per minute, chosen by the patients themselves but decided with the guidance of an expert. It is recommended that the level of sound does not exceed 60 decibels, and the music should not have lyrics (4).

How does music affect our brain and body?

Music stimulates many parts of our brain or prevents overstimulation. Some rhythms help with the coordination of certain parts of the brain. For instance, it is used as a supportive method to help Parkinson's or stroke patients regain their ability to move. It strengthens the memory by stimulating the memory centers, aids sleep, and reduces pain and stress. It facilitates expression of feelings and communication (5).

Music also causes emotional changes. The hearing center directly stimulates the limbic system, which is responsible for our emotions and memory. Music can stimulate the neural network as well as prevent the person from being over-stimulated. It has been shown that meditation or yoga accompanied by music slows down the breathing rate, calming the brain waves. The distinct benefits of rhythmic and harmonic moderate beats on post-operative recovery and stroke as well as Parkinson's and dementia have been proven with experiments. It is established that music and singing lowers blood pressure and reduces or stops pain by enabling the release of the happiness hormone endorphins. By lowering the heart and breathing rate along with their rhythm, it calms the person and can help in reducing anxiety, fear and stress. It reduces the severity and frequency of migraine attacks and headaches. It strengthens the immune system. It reduces hormones released when stressed, such as cortisol, which weakens the immune system. It is beneficial in the treatment of chronic fatigue and depression by increasing alpha waves in the brain. Dance and music help with body coordination by relaxing the muscles (1-5).

How is the effectiveness of music shown in medicine?

In studies exploring the effects of music in the brain, brain mapping or functional magnetic resonance imaging (fMRI) methods are used. Additional methods include EEG, which records the electric discharge of the brain, and PET, which with the use of radioactive substances shows how much glucose the brain consumes. The effect of music on blood pressure and heart rhythm can be shown by ECG monitoring. In such studies, sound signals between 10-40 Hz on the electromagnetic spectrum are used (6). Researcher John Hughes studied what he called the *Mozart effect* on epilepsy patients, showing that, using music therapy, epileptic electric currents were reduced and that periods in which the patient experienced no attacks were considerably lengthened (7). The researcher used Mozart's K448 Piano Sonata in these experiments. Also, in PET studies it was revealed that music stimulates similar regions to those stimulated by food and sex; that it inspires feelings of reward and pleasure and causes euphoria (8, 9).

Which illnesses can be treated by music?

In a wide-ranging study by Komako and his colleagues in 2014, numerous trials of music treatment were reviewed and analyzed systematically from a scientific perspective (4).

According to this scientifically valued analysis (randomized controlled meta-analysis) it was found that in many illnesses, treatment with music is an effective, cheap and easily applicable method with no side effects.

According to many studies on the effect of music on healing, it was found to be effective in the following illnesses: schizophrenia and similar disorders (10), Parkinson's disease (11) depression (12), sleep disorders (13), severe mental disorders (14).

Conditions for which music can be partially beneficial include cancer (4), advanced debilitating illnesses (15), patients in intensive care on life support (16), patients in pain (17), brain damage (18), autism (19), caesarean section patients (20), coronary and artery diseases (21), and inpatients (22).

Illnesses for which music is not sufficiently effective or that need more studies to show its effect include dementia and cystic bronchiectasis (enlargement of the lung bronchi) (4).

How can music be used in hospitals, operating theatres and intensive care units?

Music is a therapeutic method used for many centuries, which has been proved to calm patients by reducing feelings of pain and stress. However, in this century, trust in medicine based on modern technology has sidelined the benefits of music in healing in medical practice. Many benefits will be reaped if music is reintroduced as part of complementary medicine, alongside modern medicine. Research has shown that music reduces anxiety and pain in hospitals in post-operative and cancer patients, as well as in patients suffering from respiratory and lung diseases. In one of these studies it was revealed that the patients' heart and respiration rhythms returned to normal after listening to 30 minutes of music; they needed less painkilling medication and sleeping aids. Music also reduced pain levels and facilitated the patients' adaptation to the physicians and nurses. Playing relaxing music in intensive care units reduced feelings of pain, and calmed infants in the hospital and accelerated their growth (2). In the sample studies, music was found to be beneficial in patients in intensive care, agitated and delirious patients, and those suffering from pain. Treatment with music was listed in international guidelines in 2013 for intensive care as a simple, easy and safe method to aid healing and treatment (1,2,4). Also, listening to music or actively singing is shown to affect the immune system and is beneficial in asthma and cardio diseases (24-27).

What is thanatological music?

In 1970s, a music genre called thanatological music emerged which was aimed at people in the final stage of terminal diseases or those close to dying. In this music genre, the aim is to relax people close to death, create a peaceful atmosphere, and be helpful to the relatives of the patients. The music, played by harp, is usually performed by a musician trained in the subject, in the environment where the patient is, and in harmony with the patient's breathing rhythm. It is said that it has many benefits for the patient and those close to the patient (29).

In summary, music is a simple, easy, and cheap medical method used in reducing stress in preventative medicine. It is also a complementary medicine method, effective in curing various chronic and psychological illnesses or in reducing their symptoms. Its beneficial effect was also shown in hospital intensive care units. For these reasons its use in health institutions as part of preventative and complementary medicine should be further promoted, and patients should be guided in how to beneficially use music.

A Story and an Observation

Rose Garden

One day they bring a 16-year-old girl who has been in a traffic accident to the intensive care unit, in a comatose condition. Her name is Belkiz.

With her white marble complexion, long lashes, and brunette curls, Belkiz looks like a sleeping angel. Belkiz cannot breathe without the aid of a respiration machine; her body is connected to life by the life support machines. The machine pumps air, her chest rises slowly, the machine extracts, her chest deflates quietly. Belkiz can respond neither to talk nor touch. She sleeps quietly, away from the world around her.

The family is distraught. Many days and nights are spent at the hospital, chasing the doctors, swinging from hope to tears. Various therapies are tried, but Belkiz does not wake up. Days turn into weeks. Life elsewhere goes on, but Belkiz's consciousness refuses to return to earth. The grief-stricken mother is inconsolable. The nights, filled with nightmares, dreams, and prayers, seem never-ending. While Belkiz hovers between life and death, the mother's heart is beating slowly. All of sudden, a breeze blows in, easing the pain. The mother, thirsty for hope, has a dream in which her daughter Belkiz is in a rose garden, humming a tune that evokes slightly love-struck, dreamy and mysterious feelings. It is as if this tune is telling the world about Belkiz's beauty and that the world needs her beauty. A soft female voice sings the song:

Dreamy girl Belkiz
Tie your soul to your body,
your body to the roots of earth
the roots to each other
and then to the strings of your heart.

The mother wakes up in tears. Warm feelings spread through her body. The melody stays with her all day. It wanders in the nooks and crannies of her brain and gets stuck in her ears. The emotions aroused by this melody dispel the hopelessness for a while. She runs to the hospital. She asks about Belkiz. Alas, there is no change. No. Change.

As nights chase one after the other, the dream becomes a recurring one: the mother sees it in her dreams often. Every time, she wakes up with a fluttering of her heart. She bolts here and there, thinking it must have a meaning. She muses, "What is this melody about? Why is it related to Belkiz?"

She hums the melody to one of her friends involved in music. The musician tells her the melody is called "The Rose Garden," adding that it's clear Belize's soul wants to heal with this song. The musician suggests finding the song and making Belkiz listen to it.

They get permission from the doctors and play the melody to Belkiz through earphones, time and time again. Belkiz's chest, doesn't react initially, but finally starts to change the rhythm of her breathing. While the mother watches her daughter through misty eyes, she sees a teardrop welling in Belkiz's eye. She holds Belkiz's hand. Her mother's love meanders from her hand to Belkiz's body, fuses with "The Rose Garden" and, as if she'd imbibed a magical potion, Belkiz wakes up, in sobs. She removes the breathing mask from her mouth. The machine sounds an alarm. Doctors and nurses rush in and see the young girl coming back to life.

After Belkiz gains her consciousness and returns home, she talks about her dreams. The sound of qanun fills the air as she wanders in a long, delicate white dress, in a courtyard full of roses in Iran. The blue night, fragrant with rose scents, floats into the water from the fountains dancing in harmony with the melody in the ponds. They run in rivulets into the ears and hearts, connecting them all together. Ever since that day, that melody that fired her soul has added meaning to her joy of life. She embarks on enriching and healing her soul and body with music.

EPILOGUE

Statistics compiled in recent years show there is an increasing tendency among the elderly to mistrust the medical sector. Conversely, interest in alternative and complementary medicine has increased (1,2). As was explained in the preceding chapters, basic methods such as musical therapy and aromatherapy are considered a source of healing in face of the mechanical model of medical practice, buttressing the strong connection between our immune system and emotional state (3-6).

On the other hand, the connection between the patient and the physician plays a major role in ameliorating the emotional state of the patient, particularly in the treatment of mental and inflammatory diseases that are closely linked to the immune system. This connection not only concerns our immediate state of health, but also our genes and the structure of our brains (7). Many researchers emphasize that merely smiling and thinking positively can lead to surprising effects on healing. Studies have shown a direct link between movement of the white blood cells and our emotional state. There is a great need for interdisciplinary cooperation and joint research to better explain such connections and develop treatment methods based on the findings.

While current medical practices offer solutions, brokered by money and machines, to individual illnesses caused by stress and adverse living conditions, mainstream medicine does not concern itself much with the patient's daily life in terms of reducing or preventing stress.

Complementary medicine methods as a discipline could help fill this gap. There isn't sufficient teaching in medical schools on this subject yet. Also, such services are not offered systematically in medical institutions. Meanwhile, according to U.S. national health statistics, Americans spend approximately $30 billion a year on complementary medicine. Approximately 9.2% of the money spent on health by an average American goes to complementary medicine practices (9-10). By looking only at this data, one can get an idea of how much this need, the extent of which is not yet known in our country, can be appreciated.

I hope this book can be an enjoyable and memorable step forward in advancing this need.

ACKNOWLEDGEMENTS

I am grateful to my family, to my close friend Fatma Balcı Kaya for her excellent translation of chapters and the following colleagues and fellow medical practitioners for their help and support in writing, correcting, improving and publishing this book:

Scientific consultation and supervision: Specialist Med. Dr Handan Kayhan (Gazi University Genetics Department), Prof. Dr. Seref Erdogan (Cukurova University, Physiology Department), Prof. Dr. Tamer Demiralp (Istanbul University Medical Faculty, Neurophysiology Department), Prof. Dr Ishak Ozel Tekin (Karaelmas University, Immunology Department), Prof. Dr Selcuk Candansayar (Gazi University Medical Faculty, Psychiatry Department), Prof. Dr. Volkan Dayanir (Batigoz, Izmir), Prof. Dr. Meltem Soylemez (Adnan Menderes University, Faculty of Fine Arts, Art Painting Department)

Visual Graphics: Yelda Ozsunar ve Umut Ok (Chapter 1). Art illustrations in other chapters: Yelda Ozsunar and Kamil Mersin, Handan Kayhan (Picture 5.2)

Text redaction: Fulya Ozsunar Azman, Michael E. Young, Sevil Demirkapi, Ali Cem Özel

Translation into English: Fatma Balci Kaya.

Translation of poems: Yelda Özsunar and Fatma Balcı Kaya

ABOUT THE AUTHOR

Professor Dr. Yelda Ozsunar Dayanir was born in Turkey. She studied at Gazi University Medical Faculty and graduated in 1992. She completed her specialty in radiology at the same university. She carried out academic and scientific studies at Copenhagen University while doing her specialization and training, and later at Harvard University (1999-2001 and 2007), at London Great Ormond Street Hospital (2013), and in neuroradiology at the Department of Biomedical Engineering at Oxford University (2017). She was named Associate Professor in 2003 and became a Professor in 2008 at Adnan Menderes University Medical Faculty, where she currently works.

While pursuing her academic career, she contributed articles to various newspapers on popular science, environment and universities. Professor Ozsunar Dayanir is a certified member of the Board of European Neuroradiology and an active member of the Boards of Turkish Radiology, Neuroradiology, Magnetic Resonance and European Neuroradiology. She also sits on the publication committee of the European Society of Neuroradiology. In addition to these, she was on the Congress Scientific Planning Committee of the Board of European Magnetic Resonance and Biology for 2017 and 2019. Dr. Ozsunar has more than 66 international publications, mostly on neuroimaging, more than 20 national publications; numerous contributions to many national and international scientific books. So far, she referenced more than 1,100 times in Science Citation Index and is referenced more than 1,600 times in Google

Academic. Dr. Ozsunar is fluent in English and has been a guest speaker at many national and international conferences (www.yeldaozsunar.com).

ABOUT THE TRANSLATOR

Fatma Balcı Kaya was born in Cyprus. She has a Bachelor of Law degree from Ankara University and a master's degree in law from University College London. Since 2000 she has been a freelance linguist for various United Kingdom government departments.

REFERENCES

Chapter 1- UNIVERSAL SYMPHONY
1-Someda CG, Electromagnetic Wave, (2nd Ed.), 2006,
CRC Press.
2-Eagleman D, Pandora-Brain: The Story of You, 2016,
Domingo Press.
3-https://www.theatlantic.com/technology/archive/
2011/08/ 6-animals-that-can-see-or-glow-in-ultraviolet-
light/243634/ (Accessed date:12.09.2017).
4-Bora İ et al. EEG Atlası, 2016, 87-92, Nobel Press.
5-http://drjoedispenza.com/files/understanding-
brainwaves_white_paper.pdf (Accessed date: 12.09.2017).
6-https://www.brainwave-music.com/free-download.html
(Accessed date: 12.09.2017).
7-https://www.psychologytoday.com/blog/the-athletes-
way/201504/alpha-brain-waves-boost-creativity-and-
reduce-depression (Accessed date:10.09.2017).
8-Palva S. et al. New Vistas for Alpha-frequency Band
Oscillations, 2007, 150-158, Trends in Neurosciences.
9-Huerta P et al.Transcranial magnetic stimulation, synaptic
plasticity and network oscillations, 2009, Journal of
Neuroengineering and Rehabilition.
10-Klimesch W et al. Alpha Frequency Cognitive Load and
Memory Performance, 1993, 241-251, BrainTopogrophy.
11-Vialette FB et al. EEG Paroxysmal Gamma Waves
Bhramari Pranayama: a Yoga Breathing Technique, 2009,
977-988, Consciousness and Cognition.
12-Ossebaard HC. Stress Reduction by Technology? An
Experimental Study Into the Effects of Brainmachines on
Burnout and State Anxiety 2000, 93-101, Applied
Psychophysiolgy and Biofeedback.
13-Palva S et al.New Vistas for Alpha-frequency Band
Oscillations, 2007, 150-155, Trends in Neurosciences.
14-Ossebaard H. Stress Reduction by Technology? An
Experimental Study Into the Effects of Brainmachines on

Burnout and State Anxiety, 2007, 93-101, Applied
Psychophysiolgy and Biofeedback.
15-Buzsaki G. Theta Rhythm of Navigation: Link Between
Path Integration and Landmark Navigation, Episodic and
Semantic Memory, 2005, 827–840, Hippocampus.
16-Duncan WC et al. Ketamine, Sleep, and Depression:
Current Status and New Questions, 2013, 394, Current
Psychiatry Reports.
17-Tononi G et al. Sleep Function and Synaptic
Homeostasis, 2006, 49-62, Sleep Medicine Review.
18-Gruzelier J. A. Theory of Alpha/theta Neurofeedback,
Creative Performance Enhancement, Long Distance
Functional Connectivity and Psychological Integration.
Cognitive Processing, 2009, 101-109.

Chapter 2- THE BRAIN AND BEYOND
1-Lodish H et al Molecular Cell Biology, 2000, New York
2-Watson LA et al In the Loop: How Chromatin Topology
Links Genome Structure to Function in Mechanisms
Underlying Learning and Memory.2016, 48-55, Current
Opinion in Neurobiology.
3-Someda C.G Electromagnetic Waves, 2006, CRC Press.
4-Eagleman D, Pandora-Brain: The Story of You, 2016,
Domingo Press.
5-Constantinidis C etalThe Neuroscience of Working
Memory Capacity and Training, 2016, 438-449, Nature
Reviews Neuroscience
6-https://engineering.mit.edu/engage/ask-an-engineer/can-
brain-waves-interfere-with-radio-waves/ (Accessed date:
16.05.2017).
7-Tadel FF Brainstorm: A User-friendly Application for
MEG/EEG Analysis. Computational Intelligence and
Neuroscience 2011
8-Bora İ et al. EEG Atlası, 2016, 87-92, Nobel Press.

9-https://www.theguardian.com/science/2017/mar/28/ neuroprosthetic-tetraplegic-man-control-hand-with-thought-bill-kochevar (Accessed date: 12.09.2017)

10-Cheng G Humanoid Robotics and Neuroscience: Science, Engineering and Society, Frontiersin Neuro engineering, CRC Press, 2015.

11-Fagiolini M et al Epigenetic Influences On Brain Development and Plasticity.2009, 207-212, Current Opinion Neurobiology.

12-Brod S et al. As Above, So Below: Examining the Interplay Between Emotion and the Immune System.Immunology. 2014

14-Suve Y et al Neuronal Activity Modifies the Chromatin Accessibility Landscape in the Adult Brain. 2017, 476- 483, Nature Neuroscience.

15-Church D et al The Genie in Your Genes: Epigenetic Medicine and the New Biology of Intention. 2008, 449-450, The Journal of Alternative and Complementary Medicine

16- Roth TL et al Epigenetic Modification of Hippocampal BDNFDNA in Adult Rats in an Animal Model of Post-Traumatic Stress Disorder. 2011, 919-926, Journal of Psychiatric Research

17-Lipkova J et al Human Electromagnetic Emission in the ELF Band. 2005, 29, Measurement Science

18-Marenus KD Methods of Measuring Human Body Frequencies or Harmonics and Treating Conditions Based on the Resonance Phenomenon Between a Product and a Human Body's Frequencies or Harmonics, ELC Management Llc, 2010.

Chapter 3- CONSCIOUSNESS AND UNCONSCIOUSNESS

1-Freud S.The standard edition of the complete psychological works of Sigmund Freud. London: Hogarth Press, Institute of Psycho-Analysis;1899–1939.

2-Wernicke C. Grundriss der Psychiatrie. Leipzig: Georg ThiemeVerlag, 1900.

3-Jung C G, The Undiscovered Self. Barış İlhan Yayınevi 3rded

4-Plum F et al. Triune Concept of the Brain and Behaviour. Toronto: University of Toronto Press. 1974

5-Wolfe P. Brain Matters: Translating Research Into Classroom Practice. Alexandria Virginia: Association for Supervision and Curriculum Development (ASCD), 2010

6-Cüceloğlu D.Human and its behavior. İstanbul: Remzi Kitabevi, 2015

7-Plotnik R. Introduction to Psychology. İstanbul: Press, 2009

8-Öztürk MO, et al. Pschiatric diseases. 2015, Nobel Press.

9-Rajmohan V, The Limbic System. 2007, 132-139, Indian Journal of Psychiatry

10-In Search of Memory: The Emergence of a New Science of Mind 1st Edition. Boğaziçi Press, 2016

11-Sousa D. How the Special Needs Brain Learns. Thousand Oaks, Calif. Corwin Press. 2006

12-Eagleman D, Pandora-Brain: The Story of You, 2016, Domingo Press.

13-Jung CG. The Archetypes and The Collective Unconscious. Princeton University Press,1981

14-Eagleman D Pandora-Brain: The Story of You, 2016, Domingo Press.

15-Jung C G., The Undiscovered Self, Barış İlhan Press 3rded

16-Zalli A et al. Shorter telomeres with high telomerase activity are associated with raised allostatic load and impoverished psychosocial resources. 2014 Proceedings of NationalAcademy of Sciences of United States of America

17-Steptoe A et al. Enjoyment of life and declining physical function at older ages: a longitudinal cohort study, 2014, 150-158, Canadian Medical Association Journal

18-Steptoe A et al. Positive Affect and Psychosocial Processes Related to Health, 2008, 211-227, British Journal of Psychology

19-Roy et al. Association of Optimism and Pessimism with Inflammation and Hemostasis in the Multi-Ethnic Study of Atherosclerosis (MESA), 2010, 134-140 Psychosomotic Medicine

20-O'Donovan et al. Pessimism Correlates with Leukocyte Telomere Shortness and Elevated Interleukin-6 in Post-Menopausal Women. 2009, 446–449. Brain, Behaviour and Immunity.

21-Buckley T et al. Inflammatory and Thrombotic Changes in Early Bereavement: a Prospective Evaluation. 2011, 1145-1152, European Journal of Preventive Cardiology

22-Danese A et al. Biological Embedding of Stress Through Inflammation Processes in Childhood. 2011, 244-246, Molecular Psychiatry

Chapter 4- THE IMMUNE SYSTEM AND THE BRAIN

1-D'Acquisto F, Smile—It's in Your Blood. 2014, 287-292,Biochemical Pharmacology.

2-Smith E M. Neuropeptides as Signal Molecules in Common with Leukocytes and the Hypothalamic-pituitary-adrenal Axis 2008, 3-14

3-Blalock JE et al. Human Leukocyte Interferon: Structural and Biological Relatedness to Adrenocorticotropic Hormone and Endorphins. Proceedings of the National Academy of Sciences of the United States of America, 1980.

4-Blalock JE et al. Common Pathways of Interferon and Hormonal Action. Nature,1980, 406– 408,

5-Wong DL et al. Epinephrine: A Short- and Long-Term Regulator of Stress and Development of Illness; A Potential New Role for Epinephrine in Stress. Cellular and Molecular Neurobiology, 2012, 737–748.

6-Zunszain PA et al. Inflammation and Depression. 2013, 135–151.CurrentTopics in Behavioural Neurosciences,

7-Maes M et al. Depression and Sickness Behavior are Janus-faced Responses to Shared Inflammatory Pathways. 2012, BMC Medicine,

8-Tizard I. Sickness Behavior, Its Mechanisms and Significance. 2008, 87–99. Animal Health Research Review.

9-Buckley C. D. Proresolving Lipid Mediators and Mechanisms In the Resolution of Acute Inflammation. 2014, 315-327 Immunity.

10-Ortega-Gomez A et.al Resolution of Inflammation: an Integrated View. 2013, 661- 674, EMBO Molecular Medicine.

11-Kidron D et al Central Administration of Immunomodulatory Factors Alters Neural Activity and Adrenocortical Secretion. 1989, 15-27 Brain, Behavior and Immunity.

12-Gouin J P et al The Influence of Anger Expression on Wound Healing. 2008, 699-708, Brain, Behaviour and Immunity.

13-Gouin J P, Kiecolt-Glaser JK. The impact of psychological stress on wound healing: methods and mechanisms. 2011, 81-93, Immunol Allergy Clin North Am.Immunol Allergy Clin North Am.

14-Rezai-Zadeh K et al CNS Infiltration of Peripheral Immune Cells: D-Day for Neurodegenerative Disease? 2009, 462-475, Journal of Neuroimmune Pharmacology.

15-Ho R T et al. The Effect of T'ai Chi Exercise on Immunity and Infections: a Systematic Review of Controlled Trials. 2013, 389-396 The Journal of Alternative and Complementary Medicine.

16-Kobayashi H et al Mind-body, Ki (Qi) and the Skin: Commentary on Irwin's 'Shingles Immunity and Health Functioning in the Elderly: Tai Chi Chih as a Behavioral

Treatment. 2005, 113-116 Evidence Based Complementary Alternative Medicine.

17-Irwin M et al Shingles Immunity and Health Functioning in the Elderly: Tai Chi Chih as a Behavioral Treatment. 2004, 223-232, Evidence Based Complementary Alternative Medicine.

18-Hayashi T et al The Effects of Laughter on Post-prandial Glucose Levels and Gene Expression in Type 2 Diabetic Patients. 2009, 185-187, Life Sciences.

19-T. Hayashiet al. . Laughter Up-regulates the Genes Related to NK Cell Activity in Diabetes. 2007, 281–5, Biomedical Research,

20-Matsuzaki T et al. Mirthful Laughter Differentially Affects Serum Pro- and Anti-inflammatory Cytokine Levels Depending on the Level of Disease Activity in Patients With Rheumatoid Arthritis. 2006, 182-186, Rheumatology (Oxford).

21-IshigamiS et. Effects of Mirthful Laughter on Growth Hormone, IGF-1 and Substance P In Patients With Rheumatoid Arthritis. 2005, 651-657, Clinical and Experimental Rheumatology.

22-Berk L S et al. Studying the Biology of Hope: an Interview with Lee S. Berk, DrPH, MPH. Interview by Sheldon Lewis. 2007, 28-31, Advances in Mind Body Medicine.

23-Broad S et al. 'As Above, So Below': Examining the Interplay Between Emotion and the Immune System. 2014, 311-318, Immunology.

24-Li Q et al. Visiting a Forest, But Not a City, Increases Human Natural Killer Activity and Expression of Anti-cancer Proteins. 2008, 117-120, International Journal of Immunopathology and Pharmacology.

25-Li Q et al. A Forest Bathing Trip Increases Human Natural Killer Activity and Expression of Anti-cancer Proteins in Female Subjects. 2008, 45-55, Journal of Biological Regulators and Homeostatic Agents.

26-Marchant J et al. Immunology: The Pursuit of Happiness. 2013, 458-460, Nature.

Chapter 5- DNA: THE INTERNAL HIDDEN LIBRARY IN OUR BODY

1-James Watson J. DNA: The Secret of Life. Arrow Press, 2014, 166, Arrow Press.

2-Dispenza J, You Are the Placebo: Making Your Mind Matter, 2014.

3-Cong Y et al,Actions of Human Telomerase Beyond Telomeres. 2008, 725-732, Cell Research.

4-Stewart SA et al, Telomeres: Cancer to Human Aging. Annual Review of Cell Developmental Biology, 2006, 531-557.

5-Church D, Genie in Your Genes,2009, Energy Psychology Press.

6-Carey N, The Epigenetics Revolution: How Modern Biology is Rewriting Our Understanding of Genetics, 2012, Columbia University Press.

7-Corsi S et al, Epigenetics, Brain and Behavior, 2012.

8-Athanasopoulos D et al, Recent Findings in Alzheimer Disease and Nutrition Focusing on Epigenetics. 2015, 917-927, Advances in Nutrition.

9-Shewale S J et al, The Potential Role of Epigenetics in Alzheimer's Disease Etiology, Biological Systems, 2013.

10-Balazs R et al, Epigenetic Mechanisms in Alzheimer's Disease: Progress But Much to Do. Neurobiology Aging, 2011.

11-Wang J et al, Epigenetic Mechanisms in Alzheimer's Disease: Implications for Pathogenesis and Therapy, 2013, 1024–1041, Aging Research Review.

12-McKinney B et al, DNA Methylation as a Putative Mechanism for Reduced Dendritic Spine Density in the Superior Temporal Gyrus of Subjects with Schizophrenia, Translational Psychiatry.

13-Maldonado R et al, Epigenetics, Behavior and Early Nicotine, 2016, 863-864 Nature Neuroscience.

14-Us Y et al, Neuronal Activity Modifies the Chromatin Accessibility Landscape in the Adult Brain. 2017, 476-483, Nature Neuroscience.

15-Frias B et al, Neurotrophins in the Lower Urinary Tract: Becoming of Age, 553-558, Current Neuropharmacology.

16-Bazak N et al, Pre-pubertal Stress Exposure Affects Adult Behavioral Response in Association with Changes in Circulating Corticosterone and Brain-derived Neurotrophic Factor, 844-858, Psychoneuroendocrinology.

Chapter 6- BELIEVING IN THE CURE: CURING WITH PLACEBO

1-Hamilton D R, How Your Mind Can Heal Your Body, 2008, Hay House, UK.

2-Dispenza J, You Are the Placebo: Making Your Mind Matter, 2014, Ray Press.

3-Kaptchuk T J et al, Components of The Placebo Effect: a Randomized Controlled Trial in Irritable Bowel Syndrome, 999-1003, BMJ (Clinical Research Edition).

4-Kaptchuck T J et al, Placebos Without Deception: Randomized Controlled Trial in Irritable Bowel Syndrome, PLoS One.

5-Wiffen P J et al, Oral Paracetamol (Acetaminophen) for Cancer Pain, 2017, The Cochrane Database Systematic Reviews.

6-Derry S et al, Oral nonsteroidal anti-inflammatory drugs (NSAIDs) for cancer pain in adults., 2017, The Cochrane Database Systematic Reviews.

7-Brown W A, The Placebo Effect in Clinical Practicei 2012, Oxford University Press.

8-Sherman R et al, Academic Physicians Use Placebos in Clinical Practice and Believe in the Mind-Body Connection, 2008, Journal of General Internal Medicine.

9-Sauro M D et al, Endogenous Opiates and The Placebo Effect: a Meta-Analytic Review, 2005, 115-120, Journal of Psychosomatic Research.

10-Sandlerve A D et al, Conditioned Placebo Dose Reduction: ANew Treatment in Attention-Deficit Hyperactivity Disorder, 2010, Journal of Developmental and Behavioral Pediatrics: JDBP.

11-Crow R et al, The Role of Expectancies in the Placebo Effect and Their Use in the Delivery of Health Care: A Systematic Review, 1999, 1-96, Health Technology Assessment.

12-Mayberg H S et al, The Functional Neuroanatomy of the Placebo Response, 2002, 728-737, The American Journal of Psychiatry.

13-Ashar Y K et al, Brain Mechanisms of the Placebo Effect: An Affective Appraisal Account, 2017, 73-98, Annual Review of Clinical Psychology.

14-Kirsch I, Response Expectancy As a Determinant of Experience and Behavior, 1985, 1189-1202, American Psychologist.

15-Khan A et al, Are Placebo Controls Necessary to Test New Antidepressants and Anxiolytics? 2002, 193-197, The International Journal of Neuropsychopharmacology.

16-Khan A et al, The Persistence of The Placebo Response in Antidepressant Clinical Trials, 791-796, Journal of Psychiatric Research.

17-Sauro M D et al, Endogenous Opiates and The Placebo Effect: a Meta-Analytic Review, 115-120, Journal of Psychosomatic Research.

18-Delbanco T L, Commentary on 'Placebo as a Treatment for Depression', 1994, 279-280, Neuropsychopharmacology.

19-Fernandez F et al, Expectation and Dopamine Release: Mechanism of the Placebo Effect in Parkinson's Disease, 1164-1166, Science.

20-Enck P et al, New insights into the placebo and nocebo responses, 195-206, Neuron.

Chapter 7- STRESS
1-Eagleman D, The Brain: The Story of You, 2016, Domingo Press.
2-Werner A et al, Stress Challenges and Immunity in Space From Mechanisms to Monitoring and Preventive Strategies, Springer Fachmedien Wiesbaden,Buch XIII, United States.
3-Bertilsson Met al, the capacity to work puzzle: a qualitative study of physicians' assessments for patients with common mental disorders,2018, 133, BMC FamPract.
4-Giovanni L et al, Adaptive and Maladaptive Aspects of Developmental Stress,2013, Springer.
5-Engel P A et al, Complementary and Alternative Therapies for Neurology, 2017, 223-232.
6-Wong D L et al, Epinephrine: A Short- and Long-Term Regulator of Stress and Development of Illness; A Potential New Role for Epinephrine in Stress, 2012, 737-748, Cellular and Molecular Neurobiology.
7-Ulrich-Lai Y M et al, Neural Regulation of Endocrine and Autonomic Stress Responses, 2009, 397-409, Nature Reviews Neuroscience.
8-Vgontzas A N et al, Adverse Effects of Modest Sleep Restriction on Sleepiness, Performance, and Inflammatory Cytokines, 2004, 2119-2126, The Journal of Clinical Endocrinology and Metabolism.
9-Athanasopoulos D et al, Recent Findings in Alzheimer Disease and Nutrition Focusing on Epigenetics, 2016, 917-927, Advances in Nutrition.
10-Sarvottam K et al, Adiponectin, Interleukin-6, and Cardiovascular Disease Risk Factors Are Modified by a Short-term Yoga-based Lifestyle Intervention in Overweight and Obese Men, 2013, 397-402, Journal of Alternative and Complementary Medicine.

11-Yadavve R K et al, Efficacy of a Short-term Yoga-based Lifestyle Intervention in Reducing Stress and Inflammation: Preliminary Results. 662-667, Journal of Alternative Complementary Medicine.

12-Kox M et al, Voluntary Activation of the Sympathetic Nervous System and Attenuation of the Innate Immune Response in Humans, 2014, 7379-7384, Proceedings of the National Academy of Sciences of the United States of America.

13-D'Acquisto F et al, Smile—It's in Your Blood. 2014, 287-292, Biochemical Pharmacology.

14-Fredrickson B L, A Functional Genomic Perspective on Human Well-being, 110, Proceedings of the National Academy of Sciences of the United States of America.

15-D L et al, Epinephrine: A Short- and Long-Term Regulator of Stress and Development of Illness; A Potential New Role for Epinephrine in Stress, 2012, 737-748, Cellular and Molecular Neurobiology.

16-Devinsky O et al, Complementary and Alternative Therapies for Epilepsy, 2012, Springer Publishing Company.

17-Benson H et al, The relaxation Response, 1974, 37-46, Psychiatry.

18-Benson. H. Beyond the Relaxation Response: The Stress-Reduction Program That Has Helped Millions of Americans, 1985.

19-Khalsa DS, Stress, Meditation, and Alzheimer's Disease Prevention: Where The Evidence Stands. 2015, Journal of Alzheimer's Disease

20-Laviola G, Adaptive and Maladaptive Aspects of Developmental Stress. 2013, Springer.

21-Liang S W et al, Life Events, Frontal Electroencephalogram Laterality, and Functional Immune Status After Acute Psychological Stressors in Adolescents, 1997, 178-186, Psychosomatic Medicine.

22-Bargellini A, Relation Between Immune Variables and Burnout in a Sample of Physicians, 2000, 453-457, Occupational and Environmental Medicine.

Chapter 8- FEAR
1-Plamper J, Fear, 2012, University of Pittsburgh Press.
2-Schmidt L A et al, Extreme Fear, Shyness, and Social Phobia, 1999 Oxford University Press.
3-Kessler R C et al, Post-traumatic Stress Disorder in the National Co-morbidity Survey, 1995, 1048-1060, Archives of General Psychiatry.
4-Breslau N, The Epidemiology of Post-traumatic Stress Disorder: What is The Extent of The Problem? 16-22, Journal of Clinical Psychiatry.
5-Kendel E R, In Search of Memory, 2016, 496, Boğaziçi University Press.
6-McEwen B S Physiology and Neurobiology of Stress and Adaptation: Central Role of the Brain, 2007, 873-904, Physiological Reviews.
7-Romeove R D et al, Glucocorticoid Receptor mRNA Expression In the Hippocampal Formation of Male Rats Before and After Pubertal Development in Response to Acute or Repeated Stress, 2008, 160-167, Neuroendocrinology.
8-McEwen B S, Physiology and Neurobiology of Stress and Adaptation: Central Role of the Brain. 2007, 873-904, Physiological Reviews.
9-Kawamura N et al, Suppression of cellular immunity in men with a past history of post-traumatic stress disorder, 484-486, The American Journal of Psychiatry.
10-Smith A K et al, Differential immune system DNA methylation and cytokine regulation in post-traumatic stress disorder, 2011, 700-788, American Journal of Medical Genetics Part B: Neuropsychiatric Genetics.

11-Roth T L, How traumatic experiences leave their signature on the genome: an overview of epigenetic pathways in PTSD. 2014, Frontiers in Psychiatry.

12-Segman R et al, Peripheral Blood Mononuclear Cell Gene Expression Profiles Identify Emergent Post-traumatic Stress Disorder Among Trauma Survivors. 2005, 500-513, Molecular Psychiatry.

13-Zieker J et al, Differential Gene Expression in Peripheral Blood of Patients Suffering From Post-traumatic Stress Disorder, 2007, 116-119, Molecular Psychiatry.

14-Ryan J et al, Biological Underpinnings of Trauma and Post-traumatic Stress Disorder: Focusing on Genetics and Epigenetics, 2016, Epigenomics.

15-Felitti V J et al, Relationship of Childhood Abuse and Household Dysfunction to Many of the Leading Causes of Death in Adults. The Adverse Childhood Experiences (ACE) Study, 1998, 245-258, American Journal of Preview Medicine.

16-Chapman D P et al, Adverse Childhood Experiences and the Risk of Depressive Disorders in Adulthood. 2004, 217-225, Journal of Affective Disorders

Chapter 9- BREATH

1-Nair. S, Restoration of Breath: Consciousness and Performance, 2007.

2-White A, Radiation and the Transmission of Energy: From Stanislavsky to Michael Chekhov, 2009, Performance and Spirituality Number.

3-Repich D, Overcoming concerns about breathing, 2002, National Institute of Anxiety and Stress Inc.

4-Jerath R et al, Physiology of Long Pranayamic Breathing: Neural Respiratory Elements May Provide a Mechanism that Explains How Slow Deep Breathing Shifts the Autonomic Nervous System, 566-571, Medical Hypothesis.

5-Ritzve T, Behavioral Intervention in Asthma Breathing Training, 2003, 710-730, Behavior Modification, 27 (5), 710-730.

6-Mori H et al, How Does Deep Breathing Affect Office Blood Pressure and Pulse Rate? 2005, 499-504, Hypertension Research.

7-Gallego J et al, Learning in Respiratory Control, 2005, 495-512, Behavior Modification.

8-Jerath R et al, Physiology of Long Pranayamic Breathing: Neural Respiratory Elements May Provide a Mechanism that Explains How Slow Deep Breathing Shifts the Autonomic Nervous System, 566-571, Medical Hypothesis.

9-Richard P et al, Breathing Practices for Treatment of Psychiatric and Stress-Related Medical Conditions, 2013, 121-140, The Psychiatric Clinics of North America.

10-Raju P S, Comparison of Effects of Yoga & Physical Exercise in Athletes, 1994, Indian Journal of Medical Research.

11-Bijlani R A, Brief But Comprehensive Lifestyle Education Program Based on Yoga Reduces Risk Factors for Cardiovascular Disease and Diabetes Mellitus, 2005, 267-274, Journal of Alternative Complementary Medicine.

12-Bhattacharya S, Improvement in Oxidative Status with Yogic Breathing in Young Healthy Males, 2002, 349-354, Indian Journal of Physiology and Pharmacology.

13-Uma K et al, The Integrated Approach of Yoga: a Therapeutic Tool for Mentally Retarded Children: a One-year Controlled Study, 1989, 415-421, Journal of Mental Deficiency Research.

14-Telles S et al, Plasticity of Motor Control Systems Demonstrated by Yoga Training, 1994, 143-144, Indian Journal of Physiology and Pharmacology.

15-Telles S, Oxygen Consumption DuringPranayamic Type of Very Slow-rate Breathing, 1991, 357-363, Indian Journal of Medical Research.

16-Kallenbach J M, Reflex Heart Rate Control in Asthma. Evidence of Parasympathetic Overactivity, 1985, 644-648.Chest

17-Harinath K Effects of Hatha Yoga and Omkar Meditation on Cardiorespiratory Performance, Psychologic Profile and Melatonin Secretion, 2004, 261-268, Journal of Alternative Complementary Medicine.

18-Busek P, The Influence of the Respiratory Cycle on the EEG, 2005, 327-333, Physiological Research.

19-Li Q, Effect of Forest Bathing Trips on Human Immune Function, 2010, 9-17, Environmental Health and Preventive Medicine.

20-Live Q et al,Phytoncides (Wood Essential Oils) Induce Human Natural Killer Cell Activity, 2006, 319-333,Immunopharmacology and Immunotoxicology.

21-T. Reilly T et al, An Investigation of the Effects of Negative Air Ions on Responses to Submaximal Exercise at Different Times of Day, 1993, 1-9, Journal of Human Ergology.

22-Mitchell B W, Effect of Negative Air Ionization on Airborne Transmission of Newcastle Disease Virus.1994, 725-732, Avian Diseases.

23-Morton L L Differential Negative Air Ion Effects on Learning Disabled and Normal-achieving Children, 1990, 35-41, International Journal of Biometeorology.

24-Li Q et al, Visiting a Forest, But Not a City, Increases Human Natural Killer Activity and Expression of Anti-cancer Proteins. 2008, 117-127, International Journal of Immunopathology.

25-Live Q et al, A Forest Bathing Trip Increases Human Natural Killer Activity and Expression of Anti-cancer Proteins in Female Subjects, 2008, 45-55, Journal of Biological Regulators and Homeostatic Agent.

26-Franco L S et al, A Review of the Benefits of Nature Experiences: More Than Meets the Eye, 2017, 14,

International Journal of Environmental Research and Public Health.

27-Komori T et al, Effects of Citrus Fragrance on Immune Function and Depressive States, 1995, 174-180, Neuroimmunomodulation.

28-Rhinewineve J P et al,HolotropicBreathwork: The Potential Role of a Prolonged, Voluntary Hyperventilation Procedure as An Adjunct to Psychotherapy. 2007, 771-779, Journal of Alternative Complementary Medicine.

29-Grof C et al,HolotropicBreathwork: A New Approach to Self-Exploration and Therapy, Ray Press.

30-Rhinewine J P et al,HolotropicBreathwork: the Potential Role of a Prolonged, Voluntary Hyperventilation Procedure as An Adjunct to Psychotherapy, 2007, 771-776, Journal of Alternative Complementary Medicine.

Chapter 10- PERCEPTION, LIGHT AND AESTHETICS

1-Eagleman D,The Brain: The Story of You, 2016, David Eagleman, Domingo Press.

2-Land M F, The Eye: a Very Short Introduction, 2014, Oxford University Press, Oxford.

3-Anderson D P, Eye Movement: Theory, Interpretation, and Disorders, 2014, Oxford University Press.

4-Geaorg B et al,Melanopsin-expressing Retinal Ganglion Cells are Resistant to Cell Injury, But Not Always. 2017, 77-84, Mitochondrion.

5-Golombek D A et al, Physiology of Circadian Entrainment, 2010, 1063-1102, Physiological Reviews.

6-Masland R H,The Neuronal Organization of The Retina, 2012, 266-280, Neuron.

7-Gollisch T, Eye Smarter Than Scientists Believed: Neural Computations in Circuits of the Retina, 150-164, Neuron.

8-Feychting M et al, Reduced Cancer Incidence Among the Blind, 1998, 490-494, Epidemiology.

9-Pushkala K et al, Prevalence of Breast Cancer in Menopausal Blind Women, 2009, 425-431, International Journal of Medicine and Medical Sciences.

10-Hun C M et al, Measuring Light at Night and Melatonin Levels in Shift Workers: A Review of the Literature, 2017, 365-374, Biological Research For Nursing.

11-Reiter R J et al, Melatonin, a Full-Service Anti-Cancer Agent: Inhibition of Initiation, Progression and Metastasis, 2017, 18, International Journal of Molecular Sciences.

12-Mańka S et al, Immunoregulatory Action of Melatonin. The Mechanism of Action and the Effect on Inflammatory Cells, 2016, 1059-1067, Postepy Higieny Medyciny Doswiadczalnez.

13-Wojcik M et al, Melatonin as Pleiotropic Molecule With Therapeutic Potential for Type 2 Diabetes and Cancer, 2017, Current Medical Chemistry.

14-Meng X et al, Dietary Sources and Bioactivities of Melatonin, 2017, 9, Nutrients.

15-Rahnama M et al, Emission of Mitochondrial Biophotons and their Effect on Electrical Activity of Membrane via Microtubules, 2011, 65-88, J Integrative Neuroscience, Vol. 10, No. 1, ss.

16-Chatterjee A, The Aesthetic Brain: How We Evolved to Desire Beauty and Enjoy Art, 2013, Oxford University Press.

17-Pearce et al, The Cognitive Neuroscience of Aesthetic Experience, 2016, 265-279, Perspectives on Psychological Science.

18-Aharon I et al, Beautiful Faces Have Variable Reward Value: fMRI and Behavioral Evidence, 2001, 537-551, Neuron.

19-Slater A et al, Newborn Infants Prefer Attractive Faces, 1998, 345-354, Infant Behaviour Development.

20-Cunningham M R et al, Their ideas of beauty are, on the whole, the same as ours: Consistency and variability in the cross-cultural perception of female physical attractiveness, 261-279, Journal of Personality and Social Psychology.

Chapter 11- SMELL, BRAIN AND BODY
1-Classen C et al, 1994, 1st Ed., Aroma: The Cultural History of Smell. Routledge
2-Pearson H, Mouse Data Hint at Human Pheromones, 2006, Nature.
3-Wedekind C et al, MHC-dependent Mate Preferences in Humans, 1995, 245-249, Proceedings Biological Sciences.
4-Taverna G et al, Olfactory System of Highly Trained Dogs Detects Prostate Cancer in Urine Samples, 2015, 193, The Journal of Urology.
5-Kitiyakarave T et al, The Detection of Hepatocellular Carcinoma (HCC) From Patients' Breath Using Canine Scent Detection: AProof-of-concept Study, 2017, 11, Journal of Breath Research.
6-Brooks S W et al, Canine Olfaction and Electronic Nose Detection of Volatile Organic Compounds in the Detection of Cancer: AReview,2015, 33, Cancer Investigation.
7-Koo M A, Bibliometric Analysis of Two Decades of Aromatherapy Research, 2017, 10, BMC Research Notes.
8-Vilelave V C et al, What do Cochrane Systematic Reviews Say About Non-pharmacological Interventions for Treating Cognitive Decline and Dementia? 2017, 135, Sao Paulo Medical Journal.
9-PDQ Integrative, Aromatherapy and Essential Oils (PDQ®): Health Professional Version. Alternative and Complementary Therapies Editorial Board, PDQ Cancer Information Summaries, 2017, National Cancer Institute.
10-Ayaz M et al, Neuroprotective and Anti-Aging Potentials of Essential Oils from Aromatic and Medicinal Plants, 2017, 9, Frontiers in Aging Neuroscience.
11-Oley R et al, Systematic Review of Evidence Underpinning Non-Pharmacological Therapies in Dementia, 2017, Australian Health Review.

12-Greenberg M J et al, Effectiveness of Silexan Oral Lavender Essential Oil Compared to Inhaled Lavender Essential Oil Aromatherapy on Sleep in Adults: A Systematic Review Protocol, 2017, 961-970, JBI Database Systematic Reviews and Implementation Reports.

13-Lakhan S E et al, The Effectiveness of Aromatherapy in Reducing Pain: A Systematic Review and Meta-Analysis, 2016, Pain, Research and Treatment.

14-KooM A, Bibliometric Analysis of Two Decades of Aromatherapy Research, 2017, 10, BMC Research Notes.

15-FrancoL S et al, A Review of the Benefits of Nature Experiences: More Than Meets the Eye. 2017, 14, Journal of Environmental Research and Public Health.

16-Hurve M H et al, Aromatherapy for Stress Reduction in Healthy Adults: a Systematic Review and Meta-analysis of Randomized Clinical Trials, 2014, 362-369, Maturitas.

17-Jones L et al, Pain Management for Women in Labour: an Overview of Systematic Reviews, 2012, 14, The Cochrane Database Systematic Reviews.

18-Hur M H et al, Aromatherapy for Treatment of Hypertension: A Systematic Review, 2012, 37-41, Journal of Evaluation in Clinical Practice.

19-Hines S et al, Aromatherapy for Treatment of Postoperative Nausea and Vomiting, 2012, 18, Cochrane Database Systematic Review.

20-Forrester L T et al, Aromatherapy for Dementia, 2014, The Cochrane Database Systematic Review.

21-Hanoian M et al, Neuroprotective Effects of Inhaled Lavender Oil on Scopolamine-Induced Dementia Via Anti-oxidative Activities in Rats, 2013, 446-453, Phytomedicine.

22-Shimizu K et al, Essential Oil of Lavender Inhibited the Decreased Attention During a Long-term Task in Humans, 2008, 1944-1947, Bioscience, Biotechnology and Biochemistry.

23-Azizi Z et al, Cognitive-enhancing Activity of Thymol and Carvacrol in Two Rat Models of Dementia, 2012, 241-149, Behavioral Pharmacology.
24-Li Q et al, Phytoncides (Wood Essential Oils) Induce Human Natural Killer Cell Activity, 2006, 319-333, Immunopharmacology and Immunotoxicology.

Chapter 12- TOUCH AND HEALING

1-Coan J A et al, Lending a Hand: Social Regulation of the Neural Response to Threat, 2006, 1032-1039, Psychological Science.
2-Wessberg J et al, Receptive Field Properties of Unmyelinated Tactile Afferents in the Human Skin, 2003, 1567-1575, Journal of Neurophysiology.
3-Morrison I et al, The Skin As a Social Organ, Experimental 2010, 305-314, Brain Research.
4-Olausson H et al, Unmyelinated Tactile Afferents Signal Touch And Project to Insular Cortex, 2002, 900-904, Nature Reviews Neuroscience.
5-Olausson et al, The Neurophysiology of Unmyelinated Tactile Afferents, 2010, 185-191, Neuroscience and Biobehavioural Reviews.
6-Olausson H W et al, Unmyelinated tactile afferents have opposite effects on insular and somatosensory cortical processing, 2008, 128-132, Neuroscience Letters.
7-Craig A D, How Do You Feel? Interception: the Sense of the Physiological Condition of the Body, 2002, 655-666, Nature Reviews Neuroscience.
8-Craig A D, Interception and Emotion: a Neuroanatomical Perspective, 2008 Chapter 16 for the Handbook of Emotion, The Guilford Press, New York.
9-Barquilla Ávila C,Therapeutic Massage on Behavioral Disturbances of Elderly Patients With Dementia,626-635.
10-Niemi AK, Review of Randomized Controlled Trials of Massagein Preterm Infants,2017, Children (Basel)
11-Tiffany Field, Touch, Cambridge: 2001, The MIT Press.

12-Gray L et al, Skin-to-skin Contact is Analgesic In Healthy Newborns, 105, Pediatrics.

13-Jane S et al, Effects of a Full-Body Massage on Pain Intensity, Anxiety, and Physiological Relaxation in Taiwanese Patients with Metastatic Bone Pain: A Pilot Study, 2009, 754-763, Journal of Pain and Symptom Management.

14-Post-White J et al, Therapeutic Massage and Healing Touch Improve Symptoms in Cancer, 2003, 2, Integrative Cancer Therapies.

15-Wilkie D J, Effects of Massage on Pain Intensity, Analgesics and Quality of Life in Patients With Cancer Pain: a Pilot Study of a Randomized Clinical Trial Conducted Within Hospice Care Delivery, 2000, 31-53, The Hospice Journal.

16-Corner J et al, An Evaluation of the Use of Massage and Essential Oil on the Well-being of Cancer Patients, 1995, 67-73, International Journal of Palliative Nursing.

17-Koga K et al, Psychological and Physiological Effect in Humans of Touching Plant Foliage—Using the Semantic Differential Method and Cerebral Activity as Indicators, 2013, 32, Journal of Physiological Anthropology.

18-Marletta G et al, Complementary Medicine (CAM) For The Treatment of Chronic Pain: Scientific Evidence Regarding the Effects of Healing Touch Massage, 2015, 127-133, Acta Bio-medica.

19-Odendaal J S et al, Neurophysiological Correlates of AffiliativeBehaviour Between Humans and Dogs, 2003, 296-301.

20-Franco L S, A Review of the Benefits of Nature Experiences: More Than Meets the Eye, 2017.

Chapter 13- TOUCHING WITH SOUND: HEALING WITH MUSIC

1-https://www.musictherapy.org / (Accessed date: 17-10-2018)

2-J. Barr J et al, Clinical Practice Guidelines for the Management of Pain, Agitation, and Delirium in Adult Patients in the Intensive Care Unit, 2013, 263-306, Critical Care Medicine.

3- Orrin D et al, Complementary and Alternative Therapies for Epilepsy, 2012 MD Shachter Springer Publishing Company, Demos Medical.

4-Kamioka H et al, Effectiveness of Music Therapy: a Summary of Systematic Reviews Based on Randomized Controlled Trials of Music Interventions, 2014, 727-754, Patient Preference and Adherence.

5-AClair A et al, A Feasibility Study of the Effects of Music and Movement on Physical Function, Quality of Life, Depression, and Anxiety in Patients with Parkinson Disease, 2012, 49-55, Music and Medicine.

6- Trainor L J et al, The Neurobiology of Musical Expectations from Perception to Emotion, 2016, The Oxford Handbook of Music Psychology Susan Hallam, Ian Cross, and Michael Thaut.

7- Hughes J R,The Mozart Effect,2001, 316, Journal of the Royal Society of Medicine.

8- Giannouli V et al, Is There a Place For Musicin Nuclear Medicine?, 2012, 188-189, Hellenic Journal of Nuclear Medicine.

9- Brown S et al, Passive music listening spontaneously engages limbic and paralimbic systems, 2004, 2033-2037, Neuroreport.

10- Mossler K et al, Music Therapy for People With Schizophrenia and Schizophrenia-like Disorders, 2011, Cochrane Database Systematic Reviews.

11- Geretsegger M et al, Music therapy for people with schizophrenia and schizophrenia-like disorders, 2017, Cochrane Database Systematic Reviews.

12- Chan M F et al, The Effectiveness of Music Listening in Reducing Depressive Symptoms in Adults: a Systematic

Review, 2011, 332-348, Complementary Therapies in Medicine.

13- Niet G et al, Music-assisted Relaxation to Improve Sleep Quality: Meta-analysis, 2009, 1356-1364, Journal of Advance Nursing.

14- Gold C et al, Dose-response Relationship in Music Therapy for People With Serious Mental Disorders: Systematic Review and Meta-analysis, 2009, 193-207, Clinical Psychology Review.

15- Bradt J, Music Therapy for End-of-life Care, 2010, The Cochrane Database Systematic Review.

16-Bradt J et al, Music Interventions for Mechanically Ventilated Patients, 2010, The Cochrane Database Systematic Review.

17-Cepeda M S et al, Music for Pain Relief. 2006, The Cochrane Database Systematic Review.

18- Bradt J et al, Music Interventions for Acquired Brain Injury, 2010, The Cochrane Database Systematic Review.

19-Gold C et al, Music Therapy for Autistic Spectrum Disorder, 2006, The Cochrane Database Systematic Review.

20-Laopaiboon M et al, Music During Caesarean Section Under Regional Anesthesia For Improving Maternal and Infant Outcomes, 2009, The Cochrane Database Systematic Review.

21-Bradt J et al, Music for Stress and Anxiety Reduction in Coronary Heart Disease Patients, The 2013, Cochrane Database Systematic Review.

22- Drahota A et al, Sensory Environment On Health-related Outcomes of Hospital Patients, 2012, The Cochrane Database Systematic Review.

23- DellaVolpel J D et al, Is There a Role for Music in the ICU,2015, Critical Care.

24- Chanda M L et al, The Neurochemistry of Music, 2013, 179-193, Trends in Cognitive Sciences.

25-Bittman B et al, Recreational Music-Making alters gene expression pathways in patients with coronary heart disease, 2013, 139-147, Medical Science Monitor.

26-Uchiyama M et al, Music Exposure Induced Prolongation of Cardiac Allograft Survival and Generated Regulatory CD4(+) Cells in Mice, 2012, 1076-1079, Transplantation Proceedings.

27-Lu Y et al, Effects of Stress in Early Life on Immune Functions in Rats With Asthma and the Effects of Music Therapy, 2010, 526-531, The Journal of Asthma.

28- Laurel J et al, The Neurobiology of Musical Expectations from Perception to Emotion, 2016, The Oxford Handbook of Music Psychology (2 ed.) Cognitive Psychology, Cognitive Neuroscience.

29- Bradt J et al, Music Therapy for End-of-life Care, 2010, The Cochrane Database Systematic Review.

EPILOGUE

1-Jin J et al. Factors Affecting Therapeutic Compliance: a Review from the Patient's Perspective. 2008, 269-186, Therapeutics Clinical Risk Management.

2- Kairuz T et al. Identifying Compliance Issues With Prescription Medicines Among Older People: A Pilot Study. 2008, 153–62, Drugs &Aging.

3-Dantzer R. Cytokine. Sickness Behavior and Depression. 2006, 441–460. Neurologic Clinics,

4- Zunszain PA et al. Inflammation and Depression. Current Topics in Behavioral 2013, 135–51Neuroscience.

5- Schwartz M. How Do Immune Cells Support and Shape the Brain in Health, Disease, and Aging? 2013, 17587-17596, Journal of Neuroscience.

6- Rattazzi L et al. CD4(+) But Not CD8(+) T Cells Revert the Impaired Emotional Behavior of Immunocompromised RAG-1-Deficient Mice. 2013, 9, Translational Psychiatry.

7- Piras G et al. Emotional Change Associated T Cell Mobilization at the Early Stage of a Mouse Model of Multiple Sclerosis. 2013, 400, Frontiers in Immunology.

8- Acquisto FD et al. Smile—It's in Your Blood. 2014,287–292, Biochemical Pharmacology,

9- Nahin RL et al. Expenditures on Complementary Health Approaches: United States, 2012. 2016, 1-11. National Health Statistics Report,

10-https://nccih.nih.gov/research/results/spotlight/americans-spend-billions (Accessed date: 17-10-2018)

www.ingramcontent.com/pod-product-compliance
Lightning Source LLC
Chambersburg PA
CBHW070806050426
42452CB00011B/1916